STRANGE DAYS INDEED

*Autobiographical stories about
motherhood by women from Wales*

Edited by

Lindsay Ashford & Rebecca Tope

APHY

Published by Honno
'Ailsa Craig', Heol y Cawl, Dinas Powys
South Glamorgan, Wales, CF6 4AH

A catalogue record for this book is available from The British Library.

ISBN 978 1870206 839

The publisher gratefully acknowledges the financial support of the
Welsh Books Council

Cover design & typesetting: Nicola Schumacher
Cover image: Mike Brinson/The Image Bank/Getty Images

Printed in Wales by Gomer

'Nobody told me there'd be days like these
- strange days indeed.'

John Lennon
from 'Nobody told me'

Contents

Introduction

When the Honno editors first invited submissions for this collection, the working title was 'The Seven Ages of A Mother'. There was no agenda – we let Welsh women writers tell the stories they wanted to tell and this is the result.

As is natural in collections like this, people have focused on extremes, the most intense experiences of motherhood. No other relationship comes close to it for depth, breadth and sheer variety. And, yes, *strangeness*. The emotions that catch you unawares as you watch the little thing that was inside you turn into a separate person; emotions that change from moment to moment. This book is a patchwork of love, pain and guilt. It takes us from the initial decision to try for a baby right through to the anguish of losing a grown-up child.

The contributions cover this strangeness from many angles: the birth that causes so much pain and confusion that the new mother can only feel resentment and anxiety; the dramatic differences between one woman's three children; the desperation associated with a sick child; the guilt about wanting more from life than just being a mum.

We hear from a pregnant priest, a politician's wife and a teenager who got pregnant while still technically a virgin. There are stories from grandmothers, stepmothers, and women who have faced the trauma of an abortion. The kaleidoscope of emotion, the many layers from day-to-day fun to deep distress make this a collection to read again and again.

Some of the accounts are very complete, others make one wonder what happened next, or what the father's or the child's point of view was. But this is mothers talking and it reflects what happens in life: we muddle through without always knowing how it feels for the other people in the equation.

If there is an overall message, it must have something to do with the courage that ordinary women are required to display, simply by becoming mothers. Throughout history this has been so, and despite the claims of modern medicine to make birth safe and painless, these accounts make it vividly clear that nothing can ever be guaranteed. From Paula Brackston's witty account of the very real risks she took to become a mother, through Dorothy Gilmore's lovely description of bringing up a Down's Syndrome daughter, to Joyce Mollet's frank account of enduring the horror of a son in a coma – the courage of these and many others shines through.

Some women have written under pseudonyms and some names have been changed in the pieces but all of the stories told in this collection are true. Both of the editors have four children each. We've been there, and we know what it's really like. In this anthology, we have tried to strike chords with just about every aspect of these strange days indeed.

Lindsay Ashford and Rebecca Tope

A "Natural" Birth

Paula Brackston

The new midwife looked at me with fresh-faced enthusiasm. 'So,' she smiled up from my unread notes, 'are you planning to have the baby at home? A natural birth, perhaps?'

I suppose it was a fair assumption to make. This was my second baby. My first was toddling around the clinic as she spoke. My rural address and slightly hippy appearance may well have given her ideas about birthing pools and aromatherapy pain relief. I might once even have harboured such notions myself. Now all I could manage was a somewhat weary laugh. She looked taken aback, so I did my best to explain.

A few years earlier my partner and I had begun to discuss starting a family. Actually, it wasn't so much a discussion as a game of ping-pong, neither of us ready to be the one to make the Big Decision. 'Kids, then. What d'you reckon?' 'Mmm. Yes, soon.' 'No rush.' 'No. But we're neither of us getting any younger.' 'Hmm, better get on with it then.' 'Best get into shape first. Give up smoking. Drink more water.' 'OK.' 'Fine.' 'Good.' 'Pass the Shiraz.' The truth was, we were both hurtling towards forty. The prospect of children was both wonderful and terrifying. Making the Big Decision seemed beyond us. So we dithered and we went out lots and had long lie-ins and drank more than was good for us and even began to think this wasn't a bad way of life, when events, as they say, overtook us.

It started as a twinge in my leg, then it became a soreness, then complete agony. After a trip to casualty suggested I had pulled a muscle I munched painkillers, borrowed a pair of crutches, and waited for things to get better. They didn't. A week later a scan finally revealed thrombosis the length of my leg. Or should that be thromboses? Whichever, I was hospitalised and pumped full of rat poison and other such delights. Ten days later, when at last I was about to be sent home, I mentioned I was thinking of starting a family. There were dark looks between the youthful doctors at the foot of my bed. Tests would have to be done. Enough blood was extracted from me to make several black puddings before the reason for my thrombosis became clear. I have a blood condition called Leiden Factor Five. This sounded to me like some sort of sun protection. The haematologist elaborated – I was a thrombophiliac. Still this wasn't getting through. He put it in simple terms – blood like tomato soup. If I continued to smoke my chances of another thrombosis (and therefore possible pulmonary embolism/stroke/death) would increase ten per cent. If I didn't stop taking the contraceptive pill they would increase twenty per cent. If I was pregnant, the likelihood went up to seventy per cent. *Seventy per cent!* These were surely impossible odds. But no, wait, the haematologist assured me, pregnancy was possible with careful monitoring and medication. The monitoring meant half a day a week in the hospital for the duration of my pregnancy. The medication was to be an injection of blood thinners administered daily into my stomach. I could come in to the clinic to have them done, I was told, or I could inject myself. A daily forty mile round trip was out of the question. In fact, the injections were not as bad as I had anticipated, especially once I had learnt how to do them with my eyes still open.

It is strange how quickly the bizarre becomes the normal. I soon fell pregnant (I love that expression, as if I tripped over a pair of discarded socks on the landing, thudded to the ground and –oops! Pregnant!) and got used to starting my day by 'shooting up' as my partner, Simon, so quaintly put it. There was some local bruising, so that as the weeks went on my tummy began to resemble some sort of psychedelic melon, but it was a small price to pay.

The morning sickness was unpleasant but manageable,

though I may never be able to face a ginger biscuit again. With the days and weeks being crossed off at an alarming rate we decided on one last quick holiday as a couple before the little tadpole grew big enough to hop out and join us. We spent a lovely few days in London visiting friends, going out, and generally doing stuff people without babies or small children do. Quick. While there was still time. On the night before we were due to go home I began to feel unwell. At first I put it down to morning sickness, although it was past eight in the evening. But things got worse. Sickness, sweating, severe abdominal pains. None of it good when you are seven weeks pregnant. We rang the nearest hospital. There was a twelve hour wait in casualty, could we go somewhere else? We tried again. Only four hours at Ealing, good enough for us. Simon drove through unfamiliar streets at speed with me groaning on the back seat, lifting my head every so often to give directions. I have one piece of advice for anyone who might find themselves in a similar situation. Don't try it at the weekend. The world, his wife and his seven children will all be in A & E with splinters in their thumbs or suspicious looking rashes. I spent four hours on a plastic chair vomiting into a paper cup wondering if I was about to lose my baby while seemingly healthy people breezed past me to be treated. I'm sure they were in extremis, but, for heaven's sake, at least they could still walk! At last I was admitted. I was hugely relieved to be in a proper bed surrounded by people dressed as doctors and nurses. It felt like the right place to be. However, as it was Saturday night the people who could do the necessary scan to determine whether I had appendicitis or an ectopic pregnancy would not be in until the following afternoon. I was taken to a small room with peeling paint and a commode and told not to eat anything. This was no hardship. However, they decided it would be best not to give me any pain relief, in case it masked symptoms. Best for whom?!

Eventually, at six o'clock the next evening, the scan showed I did have a poisonous appendix and it would have to come out. The anaesthetist came to see me to say, very gently, that I had a fifty-fifty chance of losing my baby. Here were those nasty odds again. I should have taken up gambling. The nurses at the hospital were lovely, and I'm sure the doctors and surgeons knew their stuff, but it does not help one's confidence levels to have the wheel fall off the wheelchair you are being trundled about in. The last thing I remember before the anaesthetic claimed me was talking to my unborn child, saying 'Hold on tight, little tad. Hold on tight.'

When I came round my arms were being pinned to my sides by a particularly large male nurse, two others were standing flat against the wall, and a third was clutching a bloody nose. They kept calling my name until I calmed down. Apparently, some people react violently when surfacing from being anaesthetised. I did manage to apologise, but really all I wanted to know was if my baby was OK. Back in my room a beaming doctor told me yes, everything was fine, and I could go home in a few days. I am, of course, boundlessly grateful to the people who saved my own life and that of my baby. However, the surgery was the least of it. How I survived the hospital I'll never know. I was horribly sick and in pain for the next thirty-six hours. During this time an endless stream of uniforms trotted in and out. One screamed at me for eating toast.

'What do you think you're doing?' she bellowed, 'They're waiting for you down in surgery!'

I was stunned.

'To take out what, exactly?' I wanted to know. It seemed they had got me confused with the six foot, ginger haired, bearded, Scotsman in the next room. By the following day serious boredom had set in to the point where I picked up my notes for something to read. I was a little surprised to find they weren't mine. I tried to explain this to the next efficient looking young woman who came into my room.

'My name,' I told her, 'is not, and has never been, Abdul Aziz. I am not a man, nor am I fifty-seven, and as you can see,' I pulled back my sheets with a flourish, 'I am not wearing a scrotum support. These are not my notes!'

She gave me a pitying look, said it was all very interesting, but I'd be better off telling a nurse. Turned out she was one of the cleaners. I still worry that poor Mr Aziz had his appendix whipped out unnecessarily.

Early in my stay a nurse had forced me into a pair of full-length white stockings. This was to help avoid clotting, so I was happy to wear them, even if they did look utterly ludicrous. As I hobbled down the corridor to the toilets I passed similarly attired patients. It seemed they were standard issue. I glimpsed myself in the mirror. I don't know about motherhood ageing you, but my first pregnancy seemed to have rendered me one of the living dead within a matter of weeks. The eczema on my face had gone mad. My eyes were bloodshot. And some sneaky four-year-old had apparently been backcombing my hair while I slept. It was a depressing sight. As I hobbled back to my room I exchanged nods with an equally dishevelled woman. I smiled at her weakly.

'Hospital hair!' I said, a comment meant to indicate patient solidarity.

It was only once I'd passed her I realised she was in fact a visitor.

You can imagine how pleased I was to eventually make it back home. I should explain here that home is a thirteenth century Welsh longhouse in the Brecon Beacons. It is in the most beautiful spot, completely isolated, peaceful, and magical. At the time, though, it had no telephone, and there was no mobile signal, unless you climbed up the mountain to the third rowan tree from the fence. And the house had no electricity. Now, none of this particularly bothered us, but it was not popular with my mother. Here was her only daughter, recently rescued from a life-threatening thrombosis, fresh out of hospital and surgery, increasingly pregnant, and often alone on top of a mountain with no way of contacting anyone should another emergency occur. She came to stay a lot. Little did we realise just how more precarious things were about to get.

I have to say, despite it all, I loved being pregnant. I was the happiest I had ever been, and the near death experiences soon seemed distant memories and as nothing compared to the wonder of growing a baby and preparing to become a mum.

Autumn turned to a particularly wet winter. We live in Wales, so we're used to rain, but this was something different. One day our neighbour (who lives over a mile away) alerted us to a sinister looking crack in our lane. This is a proper tarmac, council maintained road, albeit a very narrow, twisty one. It also happens to climb up the side of the hill with a giddying hundred-foot drop on one side. The crack quickly got bigger. I swear you could see it growing. The man from the Highways department came out that very day and declared the route unsafe. This we already knew. We had to move quickly. If the road went and we did not have a vehicle the other side of the landslide we would be seriously cut off. Ordinarily we might not have minded, but it was winter, we needed coal, and gas, and my mother kept on about ambulance access. And there was the teensy matter of my getting to the hospital for all that monitoring. Simon took our battered little car and drove it down the hill. The crack was now a step. The car bumped over it. Still the rain fell. We went about our business, parking the hatchback on the 'civilization' side of the fissure, clambering above the road for a couple of hundred yards, then climbing into our road-unworthy jeep for the rest of the mile or so journey to our house. As I got bigger this whole exercise got slower. The hillside above the ruined road was slippery and uneven and steep. The jeep lacked anything resembling suspension giving a ride so bumpy even I began to fear it could bring on labour. The road, in a matter of weeks, disappeared into the valley below. It was terrifying to see, and we realised how lucky we had been to have noticed the crack before it became so dangerous. We soon adapted to our new access. The hatchback/jeep combination worked. The tricky part was carting supplies between the vehicles. We ignored the expense and bought a new wheelbarrow. Visitors became fewer, but the die-hards still made it up to see us. We borrowed a friendly farmer's quad bike to cart up coal and gas (though my mother made me promise not to get on it, much as I longed to).

That Christmas it snowed. Beautiful, crisp, deep, alpine snow under turquoise skies by day and spangled ones by night. On New Year's Eve I climbed slowly up the hill behind the house to the third rowan tree from the fence and used a borrowed mobile phone to call people and wish them Happy 2001. As I sat there on a snowy tussock in my wellies, Si's coat (by now the only one that would fit me), and a ski hat, my phone resting on my sizeable bump, I thought the world had never looked more beautiful. The moon was so bright there were perfect moon shadows, and I could see for twenty miles in any direction. I stroked my bump and whispered to my little tadpole that there was a fabulous, magical world waiting for him.

The Highways department had promised us a new road, but weeks turned into months and still I was waddling around the crevasse and rattling up the hill in the jeep. It wasn't so much getting to the hospital for the birth that bothered me; it was managing without the road with a tiny baby in car seat/pram/buggy/whatever. Repeated calls to the Council yielded nothing but more promises. Something had to be done. I went to County Hall and asked to speak to the person in charge of Highways. As luck would have it, he was available, and I was shown in. I lowered my largeness onto a plastic chair and explained who I was and why we needed our road back. Soon. In fact, sooner than soon. The Man In Charge was all smiles and placating hand gestures, but the gist of what he was saying was, we'll get round to it eventually. I told him as sweetly as I could that this was not good enough. We were not going to move out (they would surely never have repaired the road), and the baby's due date was looming. I painted him a graphic picture of what might happen if a woman with my blood condition went into labour and there were complications and the ambulance could not reach me. The Man In Charge paled. I settled deeper into my chair and said that, while I hated to be a nuisance, I was not leaving his office until I had his word the road would be fixed as a priority. Within the week, preferably. We stared at each other in silence for one very long minute and then he picked up the phone. Two days later the diggers arrived and within a fortnight we had a beautiful new road. My mother cancelled the Air Ambulance.

With the coming of spring our thoughts not unnaturally turned to Spring-cleaning. I'd heard that pregnant women take up bleaching things and scrubbing floors in preparation for the new arrival, and I have to say I never thought it would happen to me. I'm of the opinion that housework is mostly unnecessary and often downright dangerous. However, our house was an unusual case, and not in a baby friendly state by anyone's reckoning. Did I mention we had no electricity? We had managed happily with candles, pot-holer's headlamps, and a couple of gaslights, but of course we couldn't use a vacuum cleaner. And the house is very old. And the dust had lain thick for many years before I had moved in. With a burst of energy never before expended on cleaning by either of us, we hired a generator for the weekend and borrowed an industrial strength Hoover. Not that I could use the thing, as it was too heavy for me to lift, and my enormous bump prevented me bending in the middle. Anyway, several family members and a few friends arrived for the weekend with rubber gloves and crates of beer and we set to. The first shock when we switched on the generator and attached some lights was the extent of the cobwebs. I loathe spiders, and the realisation that the Hanging Gardens of Babylon that dangled from our ceiling were constructed entirely of arachnid nests was horrifying. It took two days of vacuuming, sweeping, shrieking (by me, at spiders), tearing up of rotting carpet, assembling of baby furniture, and general wiping down with damp cloth (sometimes each other) to transform our grubby home into a gleaming, baby-ready dwelling. We were so impressed with all this technology that we went out and bought a little generator all of our own. We were promptly given a washing machine, and with hindsight can see that life would have been horrendous without one once the baby arrived and set about creating Andean ranges of washing all by itself. Now we had lights and a food processor. The twenty-first century had finally arrived at our home. At least by day. At night, when the generator was switched off, I would of course end up changing nappies by candlelight, as women had done up here on this mountain in this very house for nearly seven hundred years. No doubt filled with the same awe and love for their babies, but each fervently wishing the little critter would let them get some sleep.

With the Big Day only a few weeks away I trotted off (no, make that waddled off) to see my obstetrician. Why do so many of them wear bow ties? He briefly explained my options. I could go for a vaginal delivery but should anything go wrong and a Caesarean be needed we would be in trouble, because I was on high doses of blood thinners and surgery would most likely cause me to bleed to death. Not a tempting thought. Or, I could choose an elective (rather than emergency) Caesarean. They would have me in the night before, take me off the blood thinners, watch me closely to make sure I wasn't going to clot and pop my clogs before the main event, then carry out the procedure under a general anaesthetic. So much for breathing techniques and playing your favourite tunes. An epidural was possible, but in my case could lead to permanent damage of the spine. It all sounded a bit bleak. Still, the little chap was well beyond a tadpole now and had to get out somehow. I opted for the planned Caesarean and came away thinking my obstetrician was a genius for making me feel I had any choice in the matter at all.

In fact, the whole procedure was very much like having my appendix taken out, though without the feeling poisoned bit. I was given lots of morphine and spent my first twenty-four hours as a mother more stoned than I have ever been in my life. When I was finally able to focus I saw in my arms this gorgeous, bright, strong little boy, and I knew I'd do it all again in an instant. It wasn't the pregnancy I'd imagined, and it wasn't the birth I had hoped for, but here was my wonderful son and nothing else mattered. Perhaps, for me, as this was the only way I could survive a pregnancy and have a child, this was, after all, a natural birth. My son now has a sister to play with, and we have a telephone at the house and the Internet. And next summer the landlord is having electricity installed. But it is still the same magical place, and I am thrilled to be raising my babies here. We named our boy Thaddeus, which sounded like a fine and fitting name. But to us he has always been, and will always be, our little Tad.

Thief

Dee Silman

It is July 1995 and she is four years old. I am carrying her through the forest. Her long legs (she is going to be tall, like her dad) hang either side of my hip. Her arms are wrapped around my neck. She studies my profile as I talk. I am telling her a story about a princess and a bear and a witch who chases them into the woods – the sort of thing I think she will like. We won't stray too far. Her dad lies asleep in the clearing where we had our picnic. I don't think she is missing him yet.

A cracking sound in the undergrowth. We turn our heads and watch as a squirrel races up a tree. It stops halfway and we hold our breaths; it seems to look straight at us. Then it carries on, disappearing amongst the thick foliage at the top. She turns her head back to look at me, prompting me to continue. Her hair smells of bark and the earth she has been lying on. She is like a wood sprite, this child – with her bare feet and unbrushed white-blonde hair. A creature of the forest.

When we emerge into the sunshine, her dad is leaning against a log, sketching. I see it is a picture of me.

'Who is it?' he asks his daughter, holding up the pad.

'Her,' she says, pointing at me.

'And who's her?'

She smiles – a big smile that lights up her face. His smile. 'Dee,' she says. 'Dee-Dee.' Then, 'Draw *me*! Draw *me*!' He agrees and she dances off, her summer dress billowing as she spins.

Later, she falls asleep on his chest and he looks across at me, to where I am lying beside them on the rug. His slow smile is almost ecstatic – *isn't she lovely*, it seems to say. *Isn't she precious?* He reaches out a hand. For a moment, I hesitate to take it.

Later, in the car mirror, I see him plant a kiss on her soft, baby cheek. She stirs in her sleep.

On this, our first meeting, I am twenty-six years old, but Nestra is only four. I have known her father for three weeks and in that time I have been gathering him to me, tugging at the invisible string that bound us from the start. Now, I feel it going slack. I feel a sharp pain, as if glass has entered my heart. The start of some sickness.

Two weeks later and I wave merrily from the window as her father gets her out of the car. She waves back. Once inside, she explores my house, taking in the pictures on the wall, the clothes in my wardrobe, the small bed made up on the floor. I try not to think that she will be reporting all back to her mum when she gets home. I let her dress up in some of my clothes. Her father calls us for dinner and we arrive in heels and feather boas. I think we are getting on fine. But at bedtime she refuses to let him go and he spends hours upstairs, reading stories, talking, taking her on trips to the toilet or to get milk. I fall asleep on the sofa after emptying the bottle of wine. Then I drag myself off up to bed.

At some point in the night, she creeps into the bed. She presses her back against his chest and his arm comes around her like an iron band. He doesn't even wake up. But the light coming in through the door shows me that her eyes are open. She lies blinking at me until I turn over and pretend to sleep.

'She likes you,' he says. But I am not so sure.

She arrives with a photograph of her parents on their wedding day. She takes it in and out of her pocket. At last, during dinner, she lays it flat on the table. She is throwing down the gauntlet. She looks straight at me. I feel like the child.

'Your mum is very pretty,' I say. But I haven't even looked at the photo. It is only later, when Nestra is in the bath with her dad, that I slip it from her pocket. Her mum has the same slanted, green eyes, the same slightly retroussé nose. But her hair is shorter and black.

The sound of Nestra being pulled from the bath and I start

guiltily, pushing the photograph back into her dress pocket. I am some kind of thief. But so is she.

'So what's she like?' – my friend Lara and I are treading water in the shallow end of the pool.

'Not what I expected. Difficult.'

'You mean she's rude to you?'

'No. Not at all.' I think for a moment. 'She's just... competitive.'

'Well, she's bound to be. It is her dad.'

'Yes, but...' I feel wretched. '...I'm the one who feels pushed out. Isn't it usually the other way round?'

'Perhaps she feels threatened. Maybe you need to find a new role to play – not just her father's new girlfriend, I mean.'

When I get home, I look up stepmother in the dictionary: *One's parent's later wife*, it says. Then: *harsh or neglectful mother*.

I decide to take a more positive approach. On Nestra's next visit I take her clothes shopping. She is a natural. I give her free rein and, although most of what she chooses to buy is pink, it looks good on her and – most importantly – she is thrilled with it.

We are walking back to the car, hand in hand, Nestra insisting on carrying the shopping bags herself when her happy chattering halts abruptly and she wrenches her hand free of mine.

'Mummy!' she shrieks and flings herself into the arms of a woman I have never seen before, except in a photo.

The discarded bags spill across the pavement, emptying their contents into the gutter. I kneel down and start to gather them up. The woman is looking down at me; Nestra balanced on her hip as if she was born to sit there. Which of course she was.

'You must be Dee,' the woman says.

I stand up. I still have to crane my neck to look up at her. 'And you're Nestra's mum.' And, as if speaking the obvious has become a disease: 'We've just been shopping.'

She nods. 'So I see.' There is a moment where neither of us

knows what to say.

Nestra is watching it all intently.

Finally, Nestra's mum turns to her and, rubbing her nose gently with her own, says quietly, 'off you go then, fluffy duck, time for mummy to get on.'

'No!' Nestra refuses to be put down, and clings more tightly around her mother's neck.

'But Daddy will be waiting for you.'

'I want to stay with *you*!'

I feel my face begin to burn and shift awkwardly from one foot to the other.

Nestra's mother deigns to look at me again. 'I suppose I *could* take her. I wouldn't want her to get upset.'

'No, of course not,' I reply. 'I'm sure her dad will understand.'

'I'll clear it with her dad.' Steely.

I hand her the shopping bags. 'She'll be wanting these.'

But she pushes them back. 'No, you keep them. Nestra can use them as dressing up clothes when she comes to stay.' I look at Nestra, but her face is as impassive as her mother's.

'Kiss Dee goodbye,' Nestra is instructed. But her lips barely brush my cheek.

When I get back to my car, I sit for a moment, gripping the steering wheel. I try to think what it is that I am reminded of in the scene of Nestra with her mother. Then I have it: a ventriloquist's dummy. Nestra's mouth pulled into a smile that doesn't reach her eyes. Her arm stiffly waving, as if controlled by strings at her back.

I shiver. This competition is more peopled than I think. When I get home, I look up 'step': *Surface provided or utilized for placing foot on.*

September 27th 2000.

Nestra is ten years old today. I wait for her to arrive with my usual mixture of hope and reluctance.

It is a longer drive for her father now. We moved north a year ago, but he still fetches her every weekend and never complains about the drive. He is a good dad to her. Everyone says so.

When Nestra appears, she greets the dog first, as always. She has never quite forgiven her dad for getting him for me instead of for her. A small victory on my part. I would have preferred a real baby.

'Happy birthday,' I say, when she notices me standing in the doorway. I give her a squeeze and beckon her into the kitchen where I have wrapped up her presents and laid them all out on the table. There are sandwiches and cake, too.

We all sit and chat for a few minutes. Then she begins to unwrap the gifts. I can tell she appreciates the CDs. But it is harder to gauge her feelings about the diary and the pyjamas. It is obvious her dad didn't choose them. I get the feeling I have overstepped the line, somehow. Intruded on another's territory. We save the CD player until last. Nestra and her father disappear into her room for the next half hour setting it up.

I sit and eat another slice of cake, then disappear out the back door to have a smoke. I have tried a few times to give up. But cigarettes are one of the last things that belong just to me.

When I met Nestra's father, he professed to like the scent of tobacco, mixing with my perfume and the red wine we drank in copious amounts. I'm not sure he feels the same about it now.

The dog comes and sits with me and we both stare out into the garden, our bums in the house, our feet on the patio, half-in, half-out.

'If you don't like it, you should leave,' he shouted at me last night. He always says that.

'She's your daughter, not mine.'

I always say that.

I don't know how we got into such a rut. We say such unforgivable things.

'I *have* a child. I don't want any more. And neither does she.'

The dog sighs heavily and rests his snout on his paws. I flick my cigarette butt into the garden.

As I walk past Nestra's bedroom, I hear them laughing together. The pain in my chest is just an old shrapnel wound now. I go into the bathroom and run the bath. I spend a lot of time in the bath when Nestra is here.

The next day, her father is called in to work and Nestra spends all morning in bed, reading. I knock a couple of times, asking if she wants anything. But each time she regards me over the top of her book and declines. 'No, thanks. I'm fine.'

Always so polite.

Around mid-day, she emerges and asks if I mind if she takes the dog for a walk.

'Of course not,' I say. But just as she is about to leave, the phone rings. She drops the lead and, before I have a chance, pelts towards the living room and grabs the receiver.

'Oh, hi, dad...' I hear. 'No, nothing much.'

I hover in the doorway, a stupid smile on my face. 'Is that your dad?' I ask.

She nods, then gets up and takes the phone to her room. The door closes behind her. After about twenty minutes, I knock on her door. She is lying on the bed, reading again.

'Has he gone?' I ask, foolishly.

'Uh-huh.'

I wait, but there is nothing. 'Did he.. did he have a message for me?'

'Huh? Oh.' She turns a page. 'He said he'd probably be home by five.'

'Oh, right. Ok.'

She hasn't looked at me the whole time. I go out, closing the door gently behind me.

But when I get to the kitchen, I fling open the door on the washing machine, tear at the washing inside, and then hurl the door shut. For some reason I am furious. I stand for a minute, my heart beating, my fists bunched on my hips.

Then I become aware of someone watching me. I turn. Nestra

is standing in the doorway. She has seen it all. I hadn't even heard her come in. 'Is this for me?' she asks, motioning towards a sandwich on the worktop. I nod.

'Thanks,' she says. She hovers for a moment. Her lips are very red. *Lips as red as blood*.

I wonder, abstractedly, if she is wearing lipstick. She smiles. A smile I honestly don't know how to read. 'Do you mind if I phone my mum?' she asks, sweetly.

I bend down with my back to her and start sorting through the washing. 'You go ahead.' When I turn round again, she is gone.

That night, I lie awake in bed, anger still burning just beneath my ribcage. His breathing next to me is calm and regular. Infuriating. I have a sudden urge to kick him in his sleep. I feel mortally wounded. But why? Next door, I hear the click of a light switch and the creaking of bedsprings as Nestra rolls over in her bed. I realise I am holding my breath.

Just who is jealous of whom? I wonder.

Do Nestra and I both want the missing piece that the other has? And what is it about us that makes the missing piece seem so sweet?

September 2002.
I am six months pregnant. We are lying on a beach in France. I have dug out a hole in the sand so that I can lie on my front. Through half-opened eyes, I can see Nestra's long legs stretched out next to me. They are covered by the shade of a parasol. She has always burnt easily. *Skin as white as snow*.

When she and her father get up to go for a swim, I struggle to sit up. *Beached whale*, I think. I hope no one is watching me. I manage to turn and sit with my back against a rucksack. My child drops awkwardly between my thighs – I am like the wolf with his belly full of stones. I rest my hands either side of my belly button, palms pressed against the stretched Lycra of my swimsuit. Then I look across the hazy sand and watch their retreating figures.

She is only a head shorter than him now. They have the same swaggering walk. She reaches across and pokes him under his ribs. He moves to poke her back but she sidesteps him, her long gazelle legs kicking up the sand. He bends down and pretends to study something at his feet, then, when she comes closer, he makes a grab for her ankle and brings her crashing down. She flails about for a while as he tickles her, her shrieks reaching me after what seems to be a one or two second delay.

The baby stirs and I press my palms down as it swims beneath in its own clear sea. *Hello*, I say to it. *Hello, my precious one*.

After a few moments, I look back up. They are at the water's edge. Nestra is dipping a toe in the water. She has one hand on her hip, the other reaching to push back a strand of blonde hair. I notice several of the men on the beach looking at her. And some of the women, too.

She has suddenly blossomed this year. She is becoming a woman. With a jolt of surprise, I realise that she is beautiful. She has filled out in all the right places. Her legs no longer seem so spindly and awkward; they are more assured, firmer in their tread – they test the ground, insteps arched, calves and thighbones elegant and firm as a colt's – almost heartbreaking to watch. I cannot take my eyes off her.

When they walk back towards me after their swim, I put on my sunglasses. I want my face to be inscrutable. But when we all decide to go and I stand up, stumbling a little in the sand, I see her swift glance take me in – a practised survey from my head to my toes. The sort of strip and search that can only be inflicted by another woman. She's obviously found what she was looking for. I watch her puff out her chest a little, jut out her hip.

I hate her then. She is like a thief who waits around the corner to watch the owner walking through the threshold of his burgled house.

Later, I stand in front of the mirror in my bedroom. My legs and arms are a nuggety brown but my swollen breasts and belly shine a bright and unnatural white. I can see the beginnings of silvery stretch marks creeping like snail trails across the taut skin.

I look at my face. It is still the face of a young girl. But the expression in my eyes is one of shock. The irises are slightly blood-shot, the pupils unnaturally large. I lean further forward. I am looking for something in my own expression. The answer to some question. But I am too afraid to ask.

For the next three months, I close up like a fist. I rock my precious child inside, whispering to her day and night. She couldn't be closer. Couldn't be more secure in her cradle of skin and bone.

When the time comes, the birth is long and hard. She doesn't want to come out. Or perhaps it's me; I won't let her. I push for three hours. In the end, she has to be dragged out. They whip her away, suctioning the mucus from her lungs, massaging her tiny, pale body. But she is fine. She is more than fine. She is a miracle.

When they hand her back to me, I feel I will never let her go. She suckles on my breast, her forehead wrinkled in earnest concentration. We are still joined. The thread is tight. We sleep facing each other; with each of my out breaths, she breathes in.

October 30th 2004.

On my wedding day, I have two bridesmaids: Nestra, who is now fourteen, and my beautiful rosebud, Lila. Lila is nearly two years old. She balances on my hip as if she were made to sit there. And, of course, she was.

When I look at my favourite photograph of that day, I see recorded the transformation that has already begun to take place in all of us. I stand next to my husband in my obligatory white dress. It is carefully designed to disguise the swelling that is the four-month growth of our second child together. He is looking down adoringly at me – which is as it should be. But I am looking at Lila's sweet face. She is balanced on my hip, one chubby arm curled around my waist, but the other reaching across to grab for Nestra. She is making a bridge – between the two women she loves most in the world.

A bridge. Could it be that simple? Perhaps it could. Nestra came to see her new sister in hospital that first day.

I saw her anxious face as she watched me cradling Lila. The swift glances at her father. I suddenly knew the damage I could do; what I could steal back from her. In fact, what had already been stolen. But in my heart, I was no longer a thief.

I placed Lila gently in Nestra's arms. I watched them meet. I had been given and I was suddenly able to give.

November 2005.

Of course nothing is ever that simple. There are times when the old jealousy leaps out at me. Leaps *from* me. Because it has been planted inside and, when the circumstances are favourable, and I've been neglecting keeping it down, it still continues to grow.

And sometimes I see a return of it in Nestra's eyes. She tries to mask it quickly – she is growing up now. And we have both learnt our lessons the hard way. But mostly, like any other mother and teenage daughter, we just try to get along.

Today, Nestra and I helped Lila to make cakes. Lila sifted the flour and we helped her beat in the sugar and butter with a spoon. Then Nestra showed her how to crack the eggs. Each time the yellow yolk slid into the bowl, Lila said 'plop'. In the end, we let her use up the whole box just to hear her say it. I put the cakes in the oven and Nestra took Lila outside to play while they cooked. Then I stood at the kitchen window and watched them with the back door ajar.

The autumn leaves are thick on the ground now. The sky is heavy with mist. There is a sense of decay in the air but also an atmosphere of damp sweetness – as if the earth has started to breathe again after the long, dry summer.

Maisie wakes up from her afternoon nap and I have to go

upstairs to fetch her.

She is six months old – a beautiful, bonnie babe. Chubbier than Lila was at that age. Stronger. I sit her astride my hip, her chunky legs reaching almost to my thighs and we make our way out the back door and into the garden.

We can hear laughing coming from somewhere ahead. As we round the corner, there are Nestra and Lila kicking up the leaves. Maisie squeals with delight.

Nestra has a leaf stuck in her hair and I reach up to brush it off. Our eyes meet for a moment and we exchange a slow smile. She is still the four-year-old child I carried through the forest that day, weaving my magical tale. We have been stuck in those woods for a long time.

Perhaps finally, it is time for us to come out.

The Shadow

Irene Janes

Becoming a mother can be an honour, responsibility, privilege, blessing or a blight: sometimes spiritual, always life changing. A woman creating life can be easy, an accident or a miracle courtesy of scientists. Life as a mother may be a delight or a drudge. An everlasting adventure, or an abyss of nurturing. I make no apologies about writing about none of the above. My story encompasses a noun that few mention and not every mother experiences.

The bond between mother and son is strong, I've heard. Or was my relationship with Paul different because, unlike my first born, he wasn't in an incubator the first two weeks of his life? Back in the early seventies that meant it was two weeks before my baby felt her mother's touch or recognised me by my smell. My daughter and I were strangers when I eventually got her home. But that tale is not for now.

Paul loved his bedroom, his own space to develop. Mothers are by nature biased towards their offspring, but honestly, my boy was beautiful, brown eyes with matching freckles and a smile that could melt any heart. And so this is how I found myself, one Sunday morning, with paste brush and grey striped wallpaper in my hand. Being a full-time working mum, redecorating wasn't exactly the favourite thing on my weekend "to do" list. Paul had promised to help. I suspect that had been the incentive he knew was needed for him to get his own way. As he entered the room I saw how puberty was reshaping him: he was leaner and taller.

'Mam,' he said, weakly. 'I feel really tired and my arms are aching. I can't help, honest.' I didn't scold these teenage antics but eagerly grasped the excuse to postpone the refurbishment, so I could get on with the ironing with one less chore to do.

After lunch, which he picked at due to ulcers in his mouth, Paul lay on the sofa with his legs across my lap. The television screen showed children with bald heads. A charity was making their dreams come true. I smoothed Paul's feet, thankful for the precious gift of my two healthy children.

'There, but for the grace of God, go I,' I thought.

Unknown to me a thin trail of blood was trickling from Paul's nostril. We sat together, unaware of the onset of a silent omen.

A few days later the doctor mentioned glandular fever, a virus that can severely disrupt a teenager's hectic social life. A blood test was needed. The next morning, within four hours of this investigation, the same GP was knocking at our door. His ashen face matched Paul's.

'The hospital isn't happy with the blood sample. They want more, but Paul is to stay in this time and go straight to Ward 12, but call in to the surgery first.' The doctor hastily returned to his car, but for us, time stood still. I turned. My son was sitting halfway down the stairs grasping the banisters. We couldn't speak and our eyes locked, searching for the answers to the questions we didn't want to ask. Shocked and scared, I got a few essentials together, not knowing exactly what was needed.

Paul stayed in the car when I called in at the surgery. I was glad of those few moments on my own, to allow my fears to fleetingly surface.

Again, as with the doctor, the receptionist's limited eye contact spoke volumes, but I could not quite hear. She obviously knew something I didn't. Mutely she pointed the way to room 3. Doctor Solomon was hunched over his desk holding a brown envelope for the hospital, with my child's fate concealed inside. He confirmed the only question I asked.

'Yes, it's serious.' A word I hardly knew or understood detonated an unspeakable train of thoughts. I condemned them to the deepest corners of my mind, afraid to face what may be ahead. Things like this happened to other people's children, didn't they?

At the hospital, having a room to himself helped to defer any difficult questions my son could ask as we just talked about the advantages of not being in an open ward, with his own television and privacy.

A pleasant female registrar came to take details. I let him answer for himself. He was fifteen years old. I always seized any opportunity that would help my children on their way to adulthood and independence – sometimes motherly intervention must take a back seat. When she'd finished and left us, I made an excuse to Paul, saying I was checking the car. I tracked the young doctor to the sister's office, to find out what was wrong.

'We don't know yet. But you must realise he's seriously ill. If you come in the morning the consultant will speak to you.' This blatant contradiction did not escape me. If they didn't know what was wrong how did they know the seriousness? Everyone knew except me. Again the eyes couldn't hide it and I was happy to defer the prognosis until my mind and body were once more in sync.

Returning to Paul's room his green towelling dressing gown could no longer disguise his ravaged body. His face was drawn and as white as the pillow cradling his head. Now I could see it wasn't the transition from boy to man that had slimmed him down but a wounded body that I, his mother, his protector, had not seen. My already weakened and unravelling resolve was failing even more. I fled to the ladies' toilet and sobbed from the pain of seeing my child so ill. This was no cut knee I could kiss better.

'Be strong,' I told my reflection in the mottled mirror, which had probably witnessed this sorry scene many times before. I banged my fists on the equally veteran porcelain hand basin. But the tears didn't abate. Washing my face in cold water tenuously put me back on the road of resilience. The door flew open and broke the spell. My mother's taut face scanned mine, her arms outstretched. Briefly, I was as helpless and as needy as my own child. This should have been a precious moment between mother and daughter, but for many reasons we had never been emotionally demonstrative to each other. For the only time in our confused relationship, our maternal instincts made us peers. I pushed her away – it was too little too late. My resolve to fight for Paul was strengthening and I didn't want sporadic compassion. Something was telling me I couldn't have any false starts. I wanted to fall into her arms and cry and cry, to go back to being a little girl, with Mam making everything better, but I couldn't afford that luxury. If I was weak Paul might falter. A shadow had passed over my heart and another darker and more sinister one sat on my left shoulder. I never cried again. I tried to find solace in silence.

Alone, I kept the appointment with the consultant, Dr Choudry. The prognosis was delivered. Optimistic medical procedures described. No guarantee given.

The pit I found myself in was the colour of despair and the depth of isolation. Cowardly lurking in the shadows was the spectre named Death. The words Acute Myeloid Leukaemia echoed around my new alien world. Different words were introduced to my everyday vocabulary: chemotherapy, transplant, platelets, and bone marrow. Paul and I were being sent to a hell neither of us would return from.

Reports of Paul's disease shivered through the grapevine. I was living each parent's nightmare. Family and friends from afar came to visit. Not once did he ask what was wrong with him. How does a mother find the words to tell a teenage son his life is in the balance? His faith in his doctors was absolute. He trusted me completely and every day I had to lie to him to keep his hopes alive. Was I right? Who knows? My biggest regret is that we talked and laughed about everything except the issues that mattered. I don't mean his weight loss, collapsed veins or homesickness but the 'what ifs' that could only have negative answers. After seven weeks of treatment he was allowed home for the Christmas period.

'Wonderful, home for Christmas,' everyone said. It didn't matter if he wasn't home for Christmas, I would take it to him. All I wanted was for him to be alive. Before his temporary release from the hospital, I asked his consultant haematologist to tell Paul the diagnosis, and reluctantly he did. I was afraid to. If Paul asked questions, would I have the right answers? I don't know if he ever realised the seriousness of the situation, but to him, getting better was only a matter of time. Was I neglectful in my duty as a mother? Should I have told him his form of leukaemia was usually found in older adults and was one of the hardest to treat? I will always wonder whether, if I had, perhaps we could have talked more openly about his worst fears. But how do you prepare your child for his possible death? And at the same time keep his spirits high to see him through the horrendous treatment. I will always feel I let him down when he needed me most.

Every waking or sleeping second was geared to keeping my dear child well in body and soul. From the first day I never wore the colour of grieving, although inside I was. From my wardrobe I would only take the colours of life. I would show fate he had a fight on his hands. I was not giving in. I begged the education department for a tutor, for the days when the relentless sickness from chemotherapy abated and Paul was stronger. Passing his GCSE was not the aim but to make him think he had a life ahead of him, a future to build for, a goal.

Christmas morning dawned. My heart was heavy. Would this be his last? I wanted to run and capture this moment for eternity with a photograph. I resisted. I couldn't afford any slip ups. Everything had to be normal. He believed his illness was just an inconvenient blip in his life. But there were a few extra presents slipped into his stocking. It was as though I was caught in a hall of mirrors but reversed. Externally, I looked normal. But the internal reflections showed a distorted heart and soul. I was grieving for my seriously ill son, while putting on a smile, planning for a future that possibly would never come, and a funeral that probably would.

Four months into the illness and back in hospital for the New Year. The flow of visitors dried up. Life outside our bubble carried on as normal. We were blindfolded on a roller coaster ride.

Over the Easter weekend Paul's hair fell out due to the incessant and brutal onslaught of the intravenous chemical cocktails. His face puffed up from steroids. In 1988 baseball caps weren't in fashion and hard to find, to cover his head. A young man has his pride you know, even with a resilient disease. Around this time a bald Telly Savalas, was cast to play a television detective called Kojac, with lollipops as a prop. Thankfully, for once, the merchandisers seized the opportunity and Paul's Auntie Lynne was able to buy him a big bottle of 'Kojac lollies'.

It hurts to confess, but I only remember giving him a cuddle a few times, other than when he was retching into yet another grey cardboard kidney tray. He was an adolescent, not a mummy's boy, perhaps I was trying too hard to be a normal family, which was in a way a lifeline. Was I being selfish, putting my fears first? So many times I have since questioned the decisions I made. But not once did I say good night without telling him I loved him.

Exhaustion caused my body to stop functioning. Blacking out, I fell from the top to the bottom of the stairs. Six stitches in my head and mild concussion didn't stop me driving to see Paul in hospital the next day. It was all my doctor needed to stop me working. Up to that point I was employed in a bakery from 6.00am, finishing according to Paul's needs, depending on his vomiting, at 10.00am, or when he had tutoring, at 2.00pm. But I never left his bedside until 9 o'clock at night.

As the effects of the chemotherapy wore off his appetite became insatiable. The nursing sister drew the line when I brought in fish and chips and other patients' relatives started doing the same for their loved ones. On one occasion, when his friend visited, I supplied them both with Knickerbocker Glory glasses, tubs of various flavoured ice cream, fruit, and appropriate decorations, before retreating to the canteen. I was determined to give quality to each and every one of his days.

Although the situation was relentless, I managed to sideline the implications until June 1988, the ninth month of Paul's illness. Now the pressure was really on. The ferocious temperatures, burnt veins, drop in platelet counts, numerous blood transfusions were just a preamble for the real thing, a move to the Bone Marrow Transplant Unit at the University Hospital of Wales in Cardiff, a long way from home.

My praise for the staff could reach the furthest galaxy and back. That unit is second to none.

Isolation ward they called it. That is only a thin line from incarceration. It was a six-bed unit. Each patient, barrier nursed in their own room, not allowed to leave and only two visitors a day. I was constantly by Paul's bedside, so only one other visitor was acceptable – not that it mattered, even visits from Paul's nearest and dearest could be counted on two digits, and they were only weekly. It was Paul and me against the world and what lay beyond. Infection was one of his constant enemies. Each time before entering his room I "scrubbed up" like the surgeons. I wore my own underwear, blue cotton surgical trousers and top, a disposable theatre gown, plastic apron, mob cap, latex gloves, and wooden mules with paperlike sheathes over them. I had to repeat this procedure even if I left Paul's room to talk to a doctor or grab a cup of tea. The isolation was complete when the nurses found it easier to hand me his medication and food through the door than scrub up themselves and come in. Our remoteness was absolute in a hospital populated by thousands.

One weekend when the regular consultant was away, Doctor Griffiths, not one of my favourites, couldn't be convinced that Paul had a major problem eating without being in great pain. I constantly told the staff. Later I was told this doctor's response:

'What does she know? She's only his mother.' If you are a mother, dear reader, I don't think I need to describe the ranges of rage that this callous and ignorant remark evoked. Added to this was my frustration of not being believed and fear for Paul's well-being.

Monday morning, the return of Paul's regular doctor – and my nagging – paid off. An x-ray revealed a massive abscess pushing down on his windpipe, not a good thing to have when any infection could prove one battle too many. Antibiotics were quickly administered and Paul was saved to fight on. But in retrospect it wasn't necessarily a victory.

Then the big day came: a year to the day after he was diagnosed, the transplant came that could save his life. Bone marrow registers had been trawled, his sibling and parents tested. No match could be found. Not to be defeated, or as a learning curve, the doctors, ten days previously, had harvested, under general anaesthetic, Paul's bone marrow. Taken to the lab it was blasted with chemotherapy. While Paul had, again, the same vicious radical 'cure' pumped into his worn-down body, truly a life changing moment. There was no fanfare, just a bag holding his cleaned bone marrow being inserted onto a drip stand, like one of the many bags of blood he'd had before. I held his hand as we watched those precious drops find their way down the clear plastic tube, into his battered veins. But this was not the end. To secure a cure there would be more chemotherapy, another transplant and the added treatment of radiotherapy. He was sixteen now, a mother's consent for treatment no longer needed and I was sensing trouble ahead. Paul had had enough.

All my time was spent at the hospital. I slept in any spare room I could find and ate in the staff canteen. Thursday's only culinary option was curry, which I hated. I swallowed every ghastly mouthful to keep up my strength.

But with regard to my daughter I had gone full circle. At the age of seventeen she was again a stranger to me. When I did manage to get home, once a week, she would be in college or with friends. I could not make prior arrangements. Leukaemia was the keeper of my diary. I wrote her long letters, and phoned but it wasn't the same. I could do little to fill the gap caused by her not having a mother at home, reassuring her about her brother. I was constantly being torn in both directions. I consoled her and even justified my actions with one of my grandfather's sayings, 'If your children are drowning would you not save the one that couldn't swim?' (Another regret I can't fix.) Those fourteen months Cathryn lived through are forever lost to me. Even with my maternal grandfather's wisdom I still feel the guilt for leaving her to her own designs. As with Paul, the emotional holocaust even today is still a taboo subject with Cathryn.

Things were looking up. The mutant blood cells were at last on the run. After the final stretch of the seven-week confinement, Paul would be home for Christmas and hopefully, again, until the New Year. Up until this point festivities were the last thing on my mind, but at the hospital shop I did buy Paul a giant Christmas cracker. My car loaded up with his computer, accumulated magazines and videotapes, we headed for the M4. Bliss, both my children were under the homestead roof again. Suddenly I had everything to look forward to. Once home I gave brother and sister time to get to know each other again. I made my way to the supermarket. There were only five weeks to make this the best Christmas... ever.

I gleefully grasped the steel trolley. I had a ravenous son to cater for plus bridge-building with my daughter and a host of presents to buy. I eagerly bought all sorts of tasty treats and all my children's favourites. At the end of the last aisle I spotted them, Cadburys Chocolate Selection Boxes, the first item could now be crossed off my Christmas shopping list. I bent down for the biggest two boxes on sale. The shadow that had settled on me all those months before moved forward and was now in the periphery of my vision. Shoppers around me were going about their business, oblivious to my terror. From the very first day, when I sobbed in the hospital toilet, it chose now to deliver its message. For fourteen months I had carried it on my shoulder. The shadow shifted, stretched and said, 'You won't be needing two. Only one child will be alive for Christmas.' Then it was gone, I hoped, forever.

A passing shop assistant stopped and asked if I was all right. I just nodded in affirmation. What else could I do?

I put the boxes back, so vivid was this manifestation. My brief respite from fear and worry had ended, so real was the prophecy.

Four days later my father drove us at speed to the hospital in Cardiff. Paul lay on the back seat, his feet once again on my lap. In my hand a brown plastic bucket as every hour, on the hour, he vomited.

The details are long and painful. But that afternoon as he lay asleep in his hospital bed my head dropped into my hands. 'Oh God, I can't take any more.' I sobbed.

Ten hours later Paul was dead.

Were my prayers answered? Only it wasn't a prayer. Didn't God know that? I was exhausted from a night with no sleep and full of worry from my son's constant vomiting. When my barrel of reserves were empty I would find more, I always did, like all mothers. Why, why my prayer? He didn't need to take Paul to spare me. His paternal grandmother and her Catholic friends had spent a lot of money on Masses to plead for Paul's life – why didn't God answer theirs? Why mine, that was murmured in desperation?

Perhaps only a mother can identify with my feelings, and I look to heaven when I say, I wish Paul had died the week he was diagnosed. The treatment only prolonged the agony. Years later a nurse tried to console me by saying that what the doctors learned could have saved other lives. Unreservedly I looked at her, making it plain that what my son went through can't even justify that.

Time goes on, nearly eighteen years now. I still worry. Where is he? Is he waiting for his Mam? Does his soul still roam the earth? Is he in heaven with his four grandparents? Two years later, the night my father died I dreamt they were together in a beautiful field.

No child should go before their parents down that uncharted

road to eternity. It should be me waiting for him behind that great white light, gently guiding him to a place where there is no pain or torment.

You see, being a mother doesn't end, it's a job for life, even if they have just popped to the shop, gone to University, or left to make their own way in the world, as we did. The invisible umbilical cord is still there, even in death. Death – the noun no one likes.

As for Paul's giant Christmas cracker, it still lies in the attic. Well it's not mine to open, is it?

Virgins Can't Get Pregnant

Carol King

You could have called it the immaculate conception. It might have been the swinging sixties, but I had no idea I could get pregnant from doing what I did with the boyfriend I had at nineteen.

Ted was a medical student at Birmingham University. I was studying drama and art at a rather straight-laced ladies' college in Hereford. Only boys from the Conservative Club, the Rowing Club and Cirencester Agricultural College were allowed to come to our dances. There was no alcohol allowed and we were very tightly chaperoned. But just before one of our dances some bright spark put up a poster in the students' union at Birmingham saying there were five hundred sex-starved girls at Hereford College of Education. Ted and his mates borrowed a van to get there and that's how we met.

We'd been seeing each other for a few months when I had to give up my studies because my mother, who was a widow, was diagnosed with cancer. I got work as an unqualified teacher, but just a few months into the job I'd lost about a stone and a half in weight. I kept feeling sick and went to the doctor.

I couldn't believe it when he told me I was pregnant. I was so shocked I just said: 'You're a liar.' I explained that all Ted and I had ever done was heavy petting. I said that I was living at home and couldn't sleep with Ted because my mum was very strict and wouldn't let me stay out late. He told me that didn't matter. What Ted and I had done was close enough to the real thing to create a tiny chance of conception taking place. It turned out that my baby had been conceived on our dining room chair...

I told Ted the news over coffee and rum babas at a café in Birmingham. He was worried that I wouldn't agree to marry him. I didn't want to get married at nineteen. And at that time of my life I didn't want to have children. But I'd always planned to marry a doctor – eventually. If that makes me sound calculating, then I suppose I was, but I never thought I'd do it by getting pregnant.

The next hurdle was telling my mother. She was very good about it and said, 'If you don't want to get married we'll bring the baby up on our own.' That was quite brave in 1967.

Then we had to go and tell Ted's parents. They were horrified and blamed it all on me – said I'd seduced their son. His mother frightened the daylights out of me by saying I'd never experience pain like the pain of childbirth and I'd be closer to death than I'd ever been in my life. I found out from Ted that she had lost a child. It only lived three weeks, which is probably why she reacted so badly to the news of my pregnancy. Ted's gran was lovely, though. She put her arms round me and welcomed me into the family – she was the only one who did.

We arranged a wedding on the cheap. The reception was at a Chinese restaurant in Birmingham and afterwards we went to the theatre to see *A Funny Thing Happened On The Way To The Forum*. Then we went back to my mum's, where we were going to be living, and she came and tucked me into bed – just as Ted was getting undressed.

That was my wedding night. Technically I was still a virgin, but four months pregnant. I remember feeling quite frightened because my mum was in the next bedroom. We couldn't make any noise. In the end we took to doing it when she was out in the daytime, because we didn't like getting up to anything when she was next door. But the neighbours came round and said we hadn't drawn the curtains – so she found out anyway!

We lived with Mum until the baby was born. At the end of October Ted had gone back to university and I had a show. I'd read in a book that that meant the baby was going to come. I washed my hair and packed my attaché case and when Ted came home I told him the baby was on its way. We lay in bed holding hands, waiting for something to happen. Nothing did. The same thing happened again two days later. Ted got fed up and took me to the doctor's. The doctor said I was in slow labour and asked if I'd like an ambulance to take me to hospital. Ted said no, we'd go on the bus!

So off we went, on the bus, to Dudley Road Hospital, and when we got there, Ted said, 'Goodbye, I've got a lecture now,' and he left me.

In I walked, in a little yellow tent dress with green flowers on it, green nail varnish and my little brown attaché case. I was so frightened. I walked up to the reception desk and said: 'Excuse me, I'm in slow labour.' They gave me a bed and said someone would come and shave me. The nurse who came said she'd never shaved anyone before, so it took ages and I was terribly embarrassed.

Two days after being admitted there was still no sign of the baby. I had an x-ray and later that night something really bizarre happened. There was a very large lady in the bed opposite who was on a restricted diet. I woke up in the small hours to see a roast chicken coming through the window. Her daughter was on the other side passing food in to her – I thought I was hallucinating.

The next morning they gave me an enema and I started to be sick and have terrible diarrhoea. I got violent contractions and they kept asking me how long the gap between them was. I said: 'There isn't one.'

A woman in the next bed shouted, 'Will someone come and look after this young girl – she's dying!' At that point I thought I was. I was terrified. Eventually they took me up to the delivery room and broke my waters. All the medical students on the ward – friends of Ted's – were arguing over who was going to deliver the baby. When Robin, my son, finally emerged, they seemed more interested in the fact that the cord had knots in it than in me or my baby.

I had to be stitched afterwards and the student who did it said it was his first time. He looked at me through my splayed legs and said: 'I know you – you're Ted's wife aren't you? I play rugby with him.' I remember counting all the tiles on the wall and doing maths problems with them, willing it to be over.

Ted had wanted to be there for the delivery. In those days it was unusual for husbands to be allowed at the birth, but because he was a medical student they were going to let him. But as he was playing football that afternoon he arrived too late. He turned up with a bunch of red roses and I remember him wheeling me through subterranean corridors, hearing fireworks going off because it was Bonfire Night.

I never imagined that I'd give birth to a boy. I'd wanted a girl and she was going to be called Cindy Carol. I'd had everything knitted with a girl in mind, so Robin had to spend the first few weeks of his life wearing pink.

Two weeks after he was born we moved away from my mother's house into a flat. Despite the fact we were married, the landlady was very suspicious. She said we were too young to have a flat – that I looked twelve and Ted looked fourteen.

I went back to work six weeks later to support Ted, who was still at university. I was desperate to carry on studying myself and I decided to do A-level History by correspondence course in the evenings.

Robin developed a chest infection a couple of weeks after I'd started my course and when the doctor came round I was rocking the baby with one hand and writing a history essay with the other.

The doctor said: 'What are you doing?'

'A-level History,' I replied. 'I've done motherhood.'

Baby Mine

Marie France Jennings

As far as mother-in-law is concerned we are going shopping for a few essentials: baby essentials, to be kept in her garage until I can give up on superstition and the baby is safely delivered.

'Don't be late for lunch,' she calls to us from the front door. 'Liver and onion, and it won't wait.'

She knows I'll heave just looking at the red and bloody meat on the plate. I control my natural impulse to answer back, and squeeze John's arm, hoping the pressure of my fingers will release the words I want him to speak. They crawl out of his mouth, one at a time.

'Sorry, Mum, should have told you before.' He kicks an innocent pebble across the pathway that splits the front lawn into two small continents. 'We won't be in until tea time, later maybe.'

'What'd you mean?'

'Could be our last chance to be on our own before...' he taps a few silent notes on my drum-taut belly, 'before...'

'I see.' Lip-deep, the smile ages her by sending wrinkles up her cheeks and round her eyes. 'Well, do as you please.' She stands for a few seconds on the threshold before closing the door on the heat wave.

I imagine her rushing upstairs, throwing our bedroom window open, taking in the unmade bed, our night clothes draped on the back of a chair and the towels crumpled on the floor. What a mess, she'll tell herself in the mirror above the fireplace, that girl! But she doesn't know about the pain that gnaws at my lower back and locks all movement shut.

'You all right?' asks John.

'Fine.' I don't bother to mention my stomach riding so high it seems to compress my lungs, and I wonder if I'll ever be free again, to breathe or eat or sleep with ease.

'I think we should have told her...'

'Don't...' I shift my weight a little on the car seat. 'Not now, please.' My eyelids join in a contraction.

'It's her house, her grandchild, and ...'

'Did you put my bag in the boot?' I clamp my lips shut to suppress sharp words trying to break out.

'Course I did.' The steering wheel shines black with the sweat from his fingers. 'She means well you know, but it's been a long three months.'

'Your idea,' I remind him. 'Not mine. Never mine.' He slows down and stops at the traffic lights. 'Cheaper than renting a flat while the builder is finishing our house, you said,' I dab at the sweat on my forehead with a white handkerchief, 'and your mother wanted to keep an eye on me. Doesn't think I'll make it to motherhood, does she?'

'Let's not argue, all right?' Mouth in a sulk, eyes in a stare he negotiates a roundabout, glances in the direction of the suspension bridge and slows down. The tyres of our three year old Cortina grind the gravel outside St Michael's Maternity Hospital.

The building is covered from foundation to the line of the roof in deep green Virginia creeper, and the summer breeze setting the leaves shivering gives the illusion the house can breathe. The front door stands wide open, and from floor tiles to pale verbena walls the coolness welcomes us. We stand by the reception desk, home to a family of cuddly teddies, porcelain babies and a rectangular vase filled with pink carnations. John is about to press the "ring for attention" buzzer when a woman's voice calls to us from a room somewhere to our right. 'Be with you in a second.'

I lower myself onto a chair, the hard type, vinyl glossy, and all the better to make me sweat.

'It looks nice.' I'd like John to snap out of his mood. 'It's...' The
baby kicks me silent, John attends to a shoe lace then the other,
and when he looks at me I think he'd like to apologise but can't.
He's not generous with words, reserves them for the things that
matter like colleagues and professors, reviewing books, lectures,
and intellectual exchanges. Not me.

'Right,' the nurse wipes her hands dry on a paper towel, drops
it in a plastic bin.

'Sorry to keep you waiting.' She perches on a corner of the
mahogany desk, opens a ledger, runs her right index finger down
a list, plants a glossy pink nail on a line of black letters. 'There,
I've got you, Jennings, Marie France, lovely name. French?' I nod.
'I've been to Paris. Loved it.'

I've lost the power to smile.

'We'd better get you ready, hadn't we? And Dad can come too.'
I cringe, but John smiles back at her

'Nothing much will happen until Doctor Meredith turns
up, and...' a quick glance at the upside down watch pinned to
her bosom, 'he's not due until three. If we're lucky that is.' She
throws her head back, and a laugh ripples along her lightly
tanned throat.

I press my palms against the red plastic of the chair, ease
myself up, and stand, back arched and belly ahead. It wouldn't
take much for me to topple forward.

'Well done!' She tries to cup my elbow with her hand but I
shrug free. I resent her enthusiasm, the gold in her hair, her
twenty-something curves and the hint of pink polish on her
nails. I've bitten mine to the quick.

'I've put you in the blue room, down the corridor.' She's
carrying my bag while John trails behind, hands deep in his
trouser pockets. 'Thought you might prefer being on your own,
you know...'

I don't know.

'Your first, isn't it?' she asks John as if he is the one about to
give birth. 'So exciting!' Terrifying I'd say, but I don't, she'd be

upset. Mothers-to-be are supposed to glow, to radiate joy and contentment and here I am, swollen at the ankles, sweating from every pore, breasts distended and I need to find a toilet, fast.

'We'll wait for you,' she flicks her biro shut and open again so I know I have to hurry, 'and settle you in.'

I had not expected a large bedroom with tall windows and a view over a back garden with apple trees dotted around a majestic oak.

'I suggest you slip into a nightie and lie down for a while. Make the most of it!' God, that laugh of hers! 'I'll come back and go through a few questions with you.'

When I sit on the edge of the bed, perched high on metal legs, the mattress cover wrinkles with the sound of the plastic protector. My feet dangle over the lino, yellow to fit in with the blue sky walls.

I know that blue. Cold. Cold like the gynaecologist's voice a year ago. 'Remove your pants,' he'd said, 'lie on the couch, place your feet in the stirrups please, and don't move.' I closed my eyes the way children do, thinking if they can't see you, you can't see them either.

'Hopefully, I'll be able to assess sperm presence and mobility.'

I wasn't prepared for the cold gel he spread between my legs, nor for the metal speculum he pushed deep between the tender walls of my vagina still sticky with the fluid of the enforced morning coupling John and I had nearly failed to achieve.

'Try and relax.' It hurt. 'Nearly there.' He went deeper. I remember staring at the ceiling, following a crack to the window, and spotting a wasp trapped behind the gauzy curtain. I think it had died by the time the consultant told me I could get dressed and handed me a wad of tissues to mop up the colourless cream running down my thighs.

'It shouldn't take long.' The door closed quietly behind him. A clock ticked, a phone rang, and I tried to pray but couldn't find a god.

'Better get your husband in and discuss the results.' Because Mr Meredith kept his eyes on the file in front of him I think I knew. About the sperm. Sluggish he called them and not many of them either. 'Of course ours is a very inexact science, Mrs Jennings,' he took off his glasses, 'but I'm afraid that under the circumstances, I'd say a pregnancy is unlikely to occur.'

It did though. Even if the moment of conception had more to do with temperature charts, hurried penetration and lying still on the bed for long half hours, with a pillow under my buttocks, than with the fullness of physical release or exploded pleasure.

'Comfortable?'

The blonde is back, busies herself with a chart she clips at the end of my bed. She hasn't noticed that the contractions have stopped. Neither has John. Maybe I should tell them. I'll wait a while. It won't make much difference anyway. Mr Meredith doesn't believe in going over the due date – makes me sound like a lump of meat – and he'll induce tonight if the baby does not get a move on.

Come on, I tell the being hiding in my ballooned belly, come out so that I can hold you. I don't speak the words of course, we have our own language, my baby and I, a kind of thought transmission, something to do with being locked in a world for two. And I am torn, not physically – not yet – between remaining at one with my child and the need to know: boy or girl, to check the number of toes, and make sure it has not picked up extra chromosomes. 'After all,' mother-in-law pretends to whisper to friends and acquaintances, 'we don't know anything about her family.... do we? ...and what that baby is likely to inherit.'

I resent her because she's right. Ignorance is the legacy of the adopted: ignorance and bewilderment. 'How could you?' I ask the face on the black and white photograph I stole from my mum's desk, a few days after I forced her to own up to the truth. How could you grow a baby, have it snuggle inside you and rearrange your internal space, toss your emotions in the air, give it birth and dump it?

I struggle. I don't understand. Because I already love the child I carry, we belong, we need each other

'Have you thought of a name yet?' asks the nurse.

'Yes,' I say in conflict with John's no. Briony for him, Sophie for me, and so far no middle ground.

'Oh well, plenty of time yet!' and she squeaks her way out in her laced up shoes.

Two hours now I've been half-sitting, half-lying on the yellow cellular blanket that covers my bed. John has paced the floor so many times I can measure the room in footsteps.

'So, how are we doing?' In surgical green and white wellies Mr Meredith looks like something caught half way between a cartoon character and a moon walker.

'Nothing much,' jumps in the nurse as if I had lost the power of speech. 'No contractions, I'm afraid.'

She's not afraid. I am.

They've got me in a wheel chair, down a long corridor, into a lift where if the graffiti is to be believed Kevin fucked Tracey, Jason was here, and Jesus is coming back any minute now.

I wonder if babies know about the journey ahead, and if that's why mine is trying to hide, and if it's true my face might turn beetroot red with exploded veins when I push my child out. And what if I am like my mother and go short on love, what if...?

'On your back please.' I breathe in the man's cologne when he bends over me. Sickly sweet. Can't see his eyes behind the glasses and I don't know if he is smiling or grinning because his lips stick to the surgical mask

I shiver with the cold of the rubber sheet against my skin.

'Knees up please.' He grabs my feet and one after the other he straps them high and tight and forces my spine into a low bridge.

'It shouldn't take too long,' he says, 'but I'm afraid the procedure is going to be rather unpleasant.' He's way off course. It's a walk towards hell, the release of women's pain down the ages. He rams a metal instrument between my parted legs, and again, and a third time. My breath snags, I gasp for air, 'Stop, you'll kill my baby... stop...'

It's legalised rape.

I gag on the words, and he returns to his task. Is it him grunting or is it me?

The artificial sun of the lamp over my head bursts burning stars, and even behind closed eyelids they keep on exploding.

My belly turns to a trembling blubber mass. The membrane tears and I yell, and even now I remember the animal feel when the waters seeped under my back, and a deep current ran up and down my legs. His boots squelch. 'It should not be long now,' he says. 'I'll have you taken to the labour ward.' He snaps off the surgical gloves and pulls the gown down over my thighs. A little late to worry about my semi-nudity. The room smells of antiseptic and Jeyes cleaning fluid and the bed wouldn't look out of place in a cell.

I wait. No, *we* wait. The plural is real this time, with John by my side. He looks funny in his disposable theatre gown, the pale green draws life from his face.

I still don't know if he is with me on an emotional trip or just observing a woman giving birth. I look for his notepad, for a pen clipped to his shirt pocket, find none, and smile at him.

After the assault comes the waiting. And the pain. At first it nibbles its way along my back, and I think I can tame the creature; we play the game I learned in ante natal classes, I pant, it lets go, I count up to ten and it latches back on with its greedy mouth, but it's bearable. Without warning it leeches onto my spine, plants sharps teeth, and sucks, and my spinal chord becomes the passive conduit for a voracious fire. Soon there'll be nothing left of me. Or the child.

Fingers are busy with my mouth. 'Breathe in, and again.' Voices. Shouts. Footsteps. More hands. 'Not enough dilation... No, too early to consider a Caesarean section...' I taste the plastic of the gas and air mask and come face to face with a thick-lipped clown who laughs at me, drags me down a plunging corridor until darkness closes behind me. I wake up in an Alice's room, except that it's not shrunk, but grown bigger and the rabbit has hooked the clock to the wall in front of me, a white blob on an egg yolk wall. The hands won't stay still and I can't tell the time.

Not until tomorrow will I know about my baby in distress, about the madness of my nails that draw blood from the necks of the paramedic who carry me to the ambulance, about the ambulance flashing blue lights down the Bristol streets, about the running of feet down the hospital corridors and the oxygen tent at the ready.

I've got the present and the pain.

'Where's John?' I ask. A hand strokes my brow and I suppose it's him, in full surgical garb.

'I need the loo...'

'Quiet. Not now.' I don't know that voice, young, brittle, female.

'I need... I've got to go...'

I try to sit up but powerful fingers push me back. I am crying now, 'Please... let me...' I don't want to soil the couch, I don't want the humiliation, I don't want my baby dirty.

'You're not going anywhere, so stop it.'

Can't. Can't hold it back any longer. I push. 'It's coming, I'm sorry.'

'Christ! I can see the head.' What's John doing between my legs?

'Where's the bloody midwife?' A man this time, angry. 'You said another five hours. Forceps, where are the bloody forceps?'

Hands crawl all over my body, and I don't know what's going on inside my belly. Somebody is trying to open me up, I try to fight back with my legs and I roll my head from side to side to avoid the nightmare clown in the mask.

'Episiotomy, NOW... she's tearing.'

Cutting, shouting. 'Push, and again... Listen to me Marie France, you need to push when I tell you to. Wait...'

I grab a hand.

'Hold it and now… last one…The baby's coming, hold it and again…' There's no pain left, just a sucking sound. 'Head's out, you're doing fine… one shoulder, easy now, stop pushing.' Long pause. 'A girl!'

'Are you sure?' They lie the baby against my chest. Skin to skin. She sniffs, sighs, whimpers and I hold fingers so new the veins run red under the skin. 'Why doesn't she cry?'

'She's tired poor little mite. It's been quite a journey.'

I feel like a giant glove turned inside out. My head flops back against the birthing couch.

'She's beautiful,' whispers John. 'I'll come back and see you later.' He kisses my forehead, strokes my cheek and it's just me, my baby and faces blurred by movement and pain killers.

'We'll get you stitched up, check the baby and you'll get her back as soon as you are settled in the ward.' The room grows quiet, while outside in the corridor voices blow loud and angry. I catch odd words – risk, incompetent, danger – but fail to attach them to me. A rough hand wipes away blood and birth matter between my legs.

'Could I have something to drink?' I ask but the young man in the white coat wipes some more. 'Not now, he says, just keep still.'

It's a new sort of pain, sharp stabs; I'm turning into a piece of needlework. He doesn't break the silence. Yes he does, once, when I try and ease myself out of a cramp, 'I told you not to move.' The words bite.

If it didn't hurt so much it would be comical to have a face bobbing up and down between my legs, but I don't find it funny and am tempted to kick the man.

Laden with crinkly wrapped parcels, bunches of sweet peas, clean nighties and underwear neatly folded in plastic bags, the visitors negotiate their way round the ward. There are kisses and hugs, cooing and baby cuddling, photo taking and forbidden vanilla slices oozing with fresh cream. Every time the door swings open I force a smile and take if off again.

I keep looking at my watch. John's late. I want him to tell me my mum's on her way and that he'll pick her up from the airport in the morning. I want to know that the cot looks inviting now it's dressed in the blue and white gingham I starched and ironed last week, that telegrams have started to arrive, that he doesn't mind it's not a boy, that my dad's getting better and that he sent roses, red, dozens of them.

I've brushed my hair, dabbed a few drops of Miss Dior on the back of my wrists, and put on my new nightdress. I won't tell him I feel empty and sore and that I can't have any more pain killers because of the baby who sleeps in her plastic cot.

When John creeps in it's dark outside and beyond the murmur of traffic I can hear frogs celebrating the summer night. His shadow stretches on the wall in front of me.

'Sorry,' he whispers, 'can't stay long, it's late…'

'Yes.' I don't need to look at the time to know it's gone ten, 'very late.'

'I went to bed after lunch, you know for a nap, and I overslept, and…'

'And nobody woke you?'

'No, Mum thought I looked exhausted and…'

I wave the explanation towards the open window. 'Did she now? Poor you.' I think he gets the sarcasm because he shuffles a little, bends over the sleeping child. 'If your mother asks, do tell her we are doing fine, Sophie and I…'

'Sophie? I thought we were going to decide…'

'Yes, well, you weren't here, so, I did. Everybody likes it.' I include my ward mates – asleep and not bothered what I call my child – with my chin circling. 'They think it's cute.'

'Fine. Yes. Well, I'd better be off then, hadn't I?' He brushes my cheek with a "sleep well" on his breath, and he's gone; along the yellow and white tiles of the winding corridor, down a flight of stairs, and into the car park. A car door slams shuts, he starts the engine and drives home. To his mother.

A storm rumbles across the Downs and the trees whisper their longing for rain along the leaves parched with August heat.

I ease myself to the edge of the bed and lower my feet to reach the unstable floor. I lean over Sophie's cot, slide a hand under her head, breathe in her new born smell, lift the tiny body and hold it close to me.

I undo the top buttons of my nightdress.

Rain drops dance on the window ledge and lightning crosses the sky. Sophie snuffles and her lips latch onto my swollen breast.

'Look,' I whisper to my daughter, 'look at our world.'

I Love My Dog

Maggie Brice

Childbirth was going to be a walk in the park. I'd been to all the classes, read all the books. I'd probably get an A-star if there was a GCSE in it. The only thing that worried me as I went into hospital was my dog. I hoped she wouldn't miss me too much. I hoped the neighbours would look after her properly.

'Hush, bach, you're upsetting the other mothers,' came the midwife's entreaty much later, but I ignored her. Normally I'm the most considerate of people, but after hours of increasingly painful labour, I'm ashamed to say I didn't give a monkey's about anybody else. From twenty-first century to primeval woman in less than a day, I held back my head and howled. My son probably wished he'd been born with earplugs. It was probably one of the reasons he took so long to amble down the birth canal.

It wasn't supposed to be like this. I was going to be one of those perfect mothers who refused all medication to guarantee a trauma-free birth for their child. Pethidine? Epidural? I shuddered at the very idea. All this girl would need was deep breathing. I did the deep breathing all right, but it was into the mask attached to the canister of gas and air. And the only reason I didn't receive my full quota of the drugs on offer was because I'd left it too late in the proceedings to plead for them.

Hours later, I was on my second canister and the midwives were hoarse with shouting encouragement. I was pushing so hard my eyes were popping out. What was I doing wrong? Why didn't the thing inside me want to come out?

Eventually they said they could see its head and not to push for a bit, but I wasn't taking any chances. I wanted the monster out. If the midwife's reflexes hadn't been so good it would have shot past her and ricocheted off the wall.

What a push!

What a mistake! I won't bore you with how many stitches I needed because of it, but the total was impressive.

Before the doctor practised his embroidery, the midwife laid this blood-encrusted slippery creature on my stomach. He was born with his hand on his head and his elbow sticking out, she said. That's why he took so long to be born, the little imp! Ha ha!

Our eyes met. This was the wondrous moment when I was supposed to feel everlasting love for this miracle of nature. I maintained his unfocused gaze and felt only hate for all the pain he'd caused me.

I didn't tell anyone. Like many women before me, I now suspect, I went through the motions, accepting all the congratulations, flowers and cards that came my way, and displaying my baby for the widespread approval of visitors. Together with the certainty that I didn't love my child, another mystery troubled me – why was I deemed so much cleverer in producing a male heir than if I'd got my wish and produced a female one? I could understand the urgency in medieval times, but why in Swansea in this era of equal opportunities? It didn't make sense.

But at least I discovered the answer to another mystery of why nightclothes have to be worn at all times in hospital, even when you're not ill. On the third day, when the hormone hell that's coyly called "baby blues" hit me, I'd have put on my coat and shoes and made a run for it. Instead I sat on my bed and soaked the covers, crying at the horror of it all. My stitches had become infected and I was being pumped full of antibiotics. My son was a glutton who latched onto my nipples with all the speed and ferocity of an Exocet missile, causing them to crack and fester, and I hadn't been able to sleep because the woman in the next bed snored like an asthmatic bull. Forget sending schoolchildren on work placements to shops and factories. Allow them to do a two-week stint on a maternity ward and teenage pregnancies would become a thing of the past.

My baby studied me through the transparent wall of his cot. I think our disappointment in each other was roughly equal. I certainly didn't coo and fuss or smuggle him into my bed for illicit cuddles, like some mothers. He demonstrated his feelings when I changed his nappy by deftly targeting a stream of urine at my face. The first time it happened I gave him the benefit of the doubt, but on my third soaking I concluded it was deliberate.

Eventually my sentence was up and I was allowed home. Years later, the thought of what could have happened that first night still stops my breath. The maternity ward had been kept at a constant tropical temperature and all the mothers had slept on top of their sheets. Our babies, in the mini-greenhouses, had slept in their nappies and nothing else. In my total ignorance, it didn't occur to me to do any different when I got home. It was summer. My house was warm.

Not at half past four in the morning, it wasn't.

I awoke feeling chilly and glanced over at the cot. My son lay still. I felt a vague fluttering in my chest. Was he breathing? I couldn't discern any movement. I switched on the light and still couldn't be sure.

My heartbeat thundered in my ears as I reached out a hand to touch him and accelerated as my fingers closed round an icy arm.

I'd killed him!

I scooped his frozen body to mine, and the sudden movement shook him awake. He gathered his strength to protest and his screams rent the night air until I managed to placate him.

I'd almost killed my son. The enormity of it hit home and I couldn't stop shaking. Even with a duvet wrapped around the two of us, his cold seeped into my skin. I couldn't believe how stupid I'd been. I still can't. The episode marked a shift in my feelings towards him, from hate to guilt. Not much progress, but it was a start.

There was also admiration for his strength. The women of

ancient Sparta used to leave their newborn male children on the rooftops overnight to weed out the sickly ones. Mine would definitely have survived that ordeal.

Still no one guessed my secret. As the months passed I did everything a model mother should: kept him clean, played with him, took him regularly to the clinic and sought out other women with babies of the same age so that he could have friends. But it was all from a sense of duty.

It wasn't that I was incapable of love towards a fellow human being. I'd loved and lost more times than I could remember. Maybe it was the trauma of his birth, maybe it was the fact that I felt permanently tired – I don't know. What I did know was that I loved my dog more than I loved my child. This fact shocked me so much that I couldn't share it with anyone else. It remained locked in my heart and the key well and truly hidden.

It didn't help that he was a difficult child. Where most of my friends' children were content to sleep at some point during the day, mine demanded constant activity. When I'd exhausted every game in the house, I'd bundle him into his pushchair and walk for miles in the woods nearby. The dog was happy, my son was happy, and at least I was happy at all the weight I was losing.

One day when the weather was bright and mild, I decided to continue walking as far as the park. My son liked to watch the ducks on the pond and it meant I could have a rest on the bench while he was doing so. Once he became bored, we'd move on to the swings.

Fortune was kind. An elderly man had been saving up his crusts and the swans and ducks were squabbling over them at the edge of the pond. I watched my son as he drummed his heels in delight at the spectacle and marvelled at what a sunny child he could be when he was totally absorbed in something. Life would have been perfect for him if he'd had a rota of nannies to amuse him.

Once the man left, we headed for the play area. There were some teenagers twirling around on the roundabout, but they ignored us as I strapped my son into the baby swing. As I rocked him backwards and forwards, I suddenly became aware of a commotion behind us. A gang of older youths had arrived and the air was turning blue and the atmosphere nasty. My dog was tied to the railings, but would have been useless even if she'd been free. It was me and my child in the middle of a war.

I should have been scared. I wasn't an aggressive kind of person and I hated violence, so it was a complete shock to experience the rage that surged through my body and possessed me totally. As the gang swept closer, pushing and shoving and not caring who happened to be in their path, I placed myself in front of my son. Who did they think they were to threaten his safety? With a thunderbolt of certainty, I realised that I would kill to protect him.

'Touch him and you're dead!' said the voice in my head, as an ancient primordial power held me in its thrall.

The gang seemed unaware of our existence. I waited for the first one to stumble on top of us, but at the last moment they parted and flowed to either side, almost as if an unseen force field had divided them.

While they continued their fight into the distance, I dropped to a park bench and gasped for air. Blood was pounding in my ears and my ribcage was threatening to burst open. What on earth had just happened?

Whatever it was, I knew that it was momentous and that it had changed me.

When I recovered my senses, I grabbed my son from the swing and clung to him. I laid my face against his peach-soft cheek and covered it with tears. He wriggled in my arms and I told him that I loved him. He started to wail, and oblivious to my surroundings, I fed him. The dog became impatient and started to bark. I told her to be quiet.

I loved my dog, but now I loved someone else more.

Needlepoint

Eve Morgan

1971. He sits in my lap, malleable and trusting, as the doctor approaches with needle at the ready. I dutifully play my part in the betrayal: distracting and deceiving him with smiles and pet names. As the cruel tip pierces his dimpled arm I steel myself instinctively as if I could deaden the stab of pain that quickly shows in, fills and spills out of his shocked blue eyes. Because if I could, I would shield him from every hurt, bear this prick of passing misery and so much more on his behalf.

Holding him close, kissing damp neck curls, explaining and seeking forgiveness. 'I know, love, I know. But it's to make you strong. Keep you safe.'

And I so often think – if only there *had* been such an injection – to inoculate him against life, his personality, experience, temptation... Because it is the not knowing what made the difference that keeps me awake, still, in the dead watches of the unforgiving night. What was it that made him vulnerable? What tipped the balance? Why *him*? Could I have done more? Should I have done less? Where exactly did it go wrong? Round and round the weary thoughts plod.

I left the grammar school before taking my exams because I was pregnant. Being a teenage mum made me grow up fast. The man I loved went off with another girl, leaving me with the baby and a large debt I worked for years to pay off. But I liked working in the travel agency, and the baby – who fast became a toddler and then a young child – took every spare minute of my attention. He was often difficult.

It wasn't that my son argued, rebelled to an unusual extent or stubbornly refused to cooperate. He was – is – charming, funny and intelligent. His way has always been to seemingly agree with suggestions, succumb to entreaties, respond to discipline and convince with promises. Then he goes away and does whatever most pleases him at that moment in time. Those things are almost always self-destructive. From a young age he frustrated the well-meaning efforts of everyone who cared about him.

Just occasionally his desire was to do things that coincidentally made me happy and proud. At primary school he represented Wales at gymnastics. Watching him flying round an athletics track, winning a writing competition in a newspaper or getting noticed for the right reasons I would dare be optimistic that all would be well in the end.

I remarried when he was six. His stepfather is the only father he has ever known and has been unfailingly patient in the face of endless dramas and crises. I had another son when my older boy was eight. We moved house, county and finally country to escape the financial fallout of the miners' strike and consequent pit closures. Our finances improved dramatically. We had all the trappings of a comfortable life. I gained a degree and a career; my younger son (who has never had his fair amount of attention due to our lopsided family life) did well at school and went to university. We were luckier than so many, except for one thing.

Drugs were easy to find if you wanted them, in the 1970s. By the late 80s they were flooding into the depressed Valleys and my older son gravitated back there at the first opportunity. Like so many others, he graduated eagerly from marijuana to heroin. Since then I have trodden the careworn track of all mothers who once knew straightforward love for their child, but now have a fractured, tortured relationship with an addict. Did the drugs bring about mental instability or was there always something wrong? Were there clues that I, his mother, should have picked up and acted on? Could I have saved him?

Bad times, good times, hope, despair, lies, police, prison, suicide attempts, hospital, psychiatric wards, sleeping rough, social workers...on and on. It is not so unusual, but it *is* terrible.

He has injected heroin to such an extent that when he needs hospital treatment they can hardly find a vein that hasn't collapsed. I recall him during one episode laughing up at the emergency team, joking about being an 'old junkie'. Nothing can prepare you for the emotion of such moments.

My son the stranger. The innocent blue eyes I remember so well no longer look out at me from picture frames in the home he hasn't shared for so many years. I will not allow him to live with us any more. The instinct for self-preservation has ultimately overridden maternal considerations. He remains part, yet not part, of our family. I cannot bear to have those photographs around. They should be reminders of a happier time that present shadows can't destroy but instead the sight of them strikes me with unbearable sadness at the pointless waste of a precious life.

The dilated pupils of the world-weary man I see every week are very different. But there are occasions when I feel his puzzlement at how it has all come to this. Then I ache, despite everything, to hold him close and nurse it all better. Just sixteen years separate us and he has abused himself so badly that it looks like less.

I fully expect him to die before me, probably in the next decade. I know that should this happen it will not bring me peace of mind. He is unable to explain why he travelled the road he did, neither has any doctor, psychiatrist or counsellor ever shed any light into that unfathomable darkness. If I didn't love him it wouldn't hurt so much and the nights wouldn't be so long.

1971. He sits on my lap. I am his protector and he is so small and innocent as the needle jabs and his face crumples with incomprehension at what I am allowing to happen to him. I bury my face in his neck/the pillow and promise him it will soon be over.

All Shall Be Well

Meg White

I settled into the coach, a protective hand over the life within, and closed my eyes. In three hours, Meg, you will be one of the first women priests in the Church of England, I told myself, in three weeks a mother again.

I had woken early, gone straight to the tiny octagonal chapel. The walnut altar was drenched in a kaleidoscope of light filtered through abstract stained glass. After the bishop's address, we remained; thirty-two women waiting to make history.

'The glorious eve of Mothering Sunday,' one ordinand whispered.

Settled in the coach on the way to the Cathedral, I recalled my selection conference ten years before.

'You're how old, dear?' My interviewer, an elderly man with pale eyes, pale skin and a faded paper-grey cardigan, nodded to himself repeatedly.

'Twenty-four.' I leant forward in the threadbare armchair that dwarfed me.

'Right... Been married long?' The head continued to nod, mesmerising me so that I had to concentrate not to do the same.

'Six years.' I wound a hand into long dark hair, smiled to cover my unease.

'Ah. Well, I should have thought a nice young lady like you would be more satisfied staying at home to have babies.' It was said with such a tranquil smile, his pale blue eyes turning liquid with the romance of his own notion. My stomach lurched, but I smiled again.

I began theological training a year later, thirty-two weeks

pregnant with my first baby.

The ordination was to be a grand public spectacle, every dark shadow of the Cathedral illuminated by the world's cameras.

'Praise to the Lord,
the Almighty...'

We processed in, a chain of hope winding through the aisles. Thirty-two white- robed women each wearing a stole, individually embroidered pieces: rainbow thread crosses, diamanté-encrusted symbols of bread and wine flashing in the camera lights. The aisles were barely wide enough for the procession, so packed were the chairs on either side.

When we finally stood in an arc before the bishop I felt the baby leap inside me. 'Send down the Holy Spirit upon your servant Meg for the office and work of a priest in your Church.' The bishop's hands rested on my head.

Our stoles, previously knotted like "Miss World" banners across our torsos, were untied to hang like triumphant scarves. The cathedral erupted in Peace. The congregation surged towards us in excited greeting. Amongst them I caught sight of Ben being pulled along by Lauren, fair curls escaping in wisps from her long blue ribbon. She shook hands with everyone in her path.

'That new priest is our mummy,' she repeated over and over. I moved towards my shy seven-year-old son and confident six-year-old daughter, elated like her. I felt the baby squirm inside me again and remembered my first pregnancy, when I was at theological college.

'It's okay, Meg. The Ministry Board just needs certain reassurances.' My Director of Ordinands' voice on the phone had been breathy and defensive.

I'd stood in the cavernous hallway of my new theological college, mind reeling, trying to steady my own voice. 'Reassurances?'

'About the pregnancy. They need to be sure that you can combine studying with being a proper mother.' He'd spoken slowly, as though explaining to an idiot.

'What?' Too loud, I'd told myself. I'd glanced away from the enquiring eyes of passers by, wound my free hand into my hair, and breathed deeply. 'How am I supposed to do that? The baby's not even born yet. Do they ask all the men with pregnant wives to prove they can study and be fit fathers?'

'No, of course not, it's just a matter of thinking through how you'll manage.'

It was an unpromising start to my theological career, but at that point I had still been confident that all would be well.

It had been harder with Lauren.

'Dennis, can I have a word?'

'Of course.'

I'd spoken quietly, craning towards my tutor, aware of the students around me in the crowded narrow common room. 'I'm going to have another baby.'

'What?' Dennis started backwards, attracting interested glances. 'You're not serious, Meg! I don't want to worry you, but you'll never get a post. If I were a bishop I certainly wouldn't take you on.' How nearly right he had been.

'I've had a conversation with a representative from the Ministry Board,' the next phone call began tentatively. 'They're rather concerned that your concentration on babies must be interfering with your full participation in college life.'

'But Rob looks after Ben, and this baby won't be born till the last term, when college life is almost wound up.' I'd laid a protective hand over the secret baby, winced at the note of fear in my voice and wished I wasn't standing in the public hallway of college.

'Be that as it may, they are concerned. These people have your best interests at heart, Meg. They do feel it very important that you get a full picture of community life and they're also concerned for Ben's welfare.' He was brisk and businesslike now.

I'd closed my eyes hard. All would be well I told myself,

blinking back a stray tear.

A few weeks later I was "released" by my sponsoring diocese as though they were freeing me from bondage, rather than washing their hands of me. Five months pregnant, I started the search for a parish. The first rejection was tortuous, the second swift and blunt – the parish was not suitable for a "working mother", the letter explained, assuring me of their concern for me. By the fourth parish I'd been ready to accept anything, or so I thought until the offer letter arrived with a copy of the parish news sheet.

> *St. Helen's News*
> *I have today offered our title post to Meg. Meg, 27, is married to Rob. They have a little boy of one and Meg is expecting their second child in April. Rob stays at home with the children. The decision to offer Meg the post was a very difficult one; similar to the decision it would have taken to offer the post to a very effeminate gay male candidate, because of the perversity of her lifestyle. However, I am sure that she will make a great contribution to our life at St. Helen's*

Two weeks before Lauren was born, I found a parish.

Lauren was born on Tuesday in Easter week. This Caesarean section took longer than the first, the thick layer of scar tissue resisting the scalpel, but at last Lauren Elisabeth was born into a life-giving universe. Within two days I had an infection in the wound. In the second week, my breasts became hard and hot and ached with the fever of mastitis. Lauren systematically regurgitated the milk that I poured into her, painfully curling into tight knots of her own private discomfort. The young, newly qualified health visitor breezed in and out of my life, the latest Monsoon clothes draped over her neat, dry breasts and flat stomach.

I'd returned to college when Lauren was four weeks old,

dragging myself through morning worship each day, visible and smiling before I collapsed into my college study to wait for the day to end.

'Peace be with you,' Lauren said solemnly, bringing me back to the present. She held out a tiny hand.

'And also with you,' I echoed, beaming.

'And me,' Rosa was at my side; her plump palm grasping my new stole. 'And you!' I agreed, swinging her into my arms. She was more solid than Lauren had ever been, warm and malleable as dough, her dark hair a riot of thick curls. I swung my two year old into Rob's arms as he approached smiling.

I had been halfway through my curacy when I announced that I was pregnant for a third time. I was six months pregnant before an ad hoc arrangement for leave was reached; a 'maternity policy' it was felt, would be going a little too far.

An eternity passed under the glare of hospital lights while the epidural was inserted, and another eternity before there was a cry and the glimpse of a baby being whisked away. Rosa was a beautiful baby – round faced, eyes that were the darkest pools of clear, midnight blue, the devastating fragility and enormous strength of new life. I loved her immediately, a comfortable, well-worn love for someone I'd known for a very long time.

But there was an uneasiness in the parish after the maternity leave. Although I had nearly two years to go on my curacy, my Archdeacon decided, without explanation, that it might be best if I move on and sent me on a wild goose chase of impossible parishes. The last one had a woman deacon already in post and I was grateful that I decided to defy my Archdeacon to talk to her.

'I believe you're leaving,' I began cautiously. Rosa was asleep on the sofa at my side, soft and dark. Outside Ben and Lauren were blowing bubbles in the garden, warmly wrapped against the chill spring air. I stroked Rosa with one finger as I talked, curling into the big red sofa that took up most of our tiny living room.

'Certainly am, the sooner the better.' The voice on the other end was eager to divulge.

'Would you mind telling me a bit?' Rosa stirred slightly and I placed a hand on her arm, nestled closer to her.

'It's been hell from the start. There's this charming Non-Stipendiary Minister – misogyny really doesn't say it. Let's put it this way, my vicar has promised him faithfully that any woman curate here will never be priested no matter what Synod decides.'

I gulped, I had no idea how long it might take for Synod to decide to allow women to be priested, but I wanted to be ready when the call came. 'Sounds appalling.' I twisted a hand into my hair anxiously.

'You've heard nothing yet,' continued Tara, grateful to pour it all out to anyone. 'I had maternity leave last year…'

'I'm on maternity leave at the moment.'

'I had twins, total shock. Anyway, while I was away, the Church Council decided that I couldn't possibly work full–time with two babies so I could only come back part-time. No consultation, nothing. They got the bishop's agreement before they even sprang it on me.'

'What?'

'Part-time indeed! Forty hours a week for £5,000 a year! My husband had given in his notice to look after the twins, so you can imagine what it's been like for us.'

'It's unbelievable!' I sat upright, wound my hand tighter into my hair.

'You'd better believe it or they'll have you for breakfast too.'

'So what are you going to do?'

'Give up. Tom's got a job and we're moving out of London. Don't mind if I never see the inside of a church or vicarage again.'

'Oh Tara!'

'Just don't come here.'

The Archdeacon sounded flustered when he next rang; 'James Lockley says he hasn't heard from you yet —' he began curtly.

'No, I was going to ring you. I really don't think St. Mark's is for me.' I wound my hand into my hair, steadied my voice.

'But you haven't looked at it!'

'I spoke to Tara,' I felt determined. I was not going to take my babies to live in a place like that.

'I did warn you that that wouldn't be helpful.'

'She was very helpful, actually. I'm not very happy about working with colleagues opposed to women's ordination.'

'Not James, he'd be very supportive,' the voice was terse.

'Tara says he's agreed with the Non-Stipendiary that no woman deacon could ever be priested in that parish.'

'Well, yes, but for practical purposes...' the voice was smoother now, oily, but I was not going to be persuaded.

'I'm sorry, that's not what I call supportive. I also understand that the parish is not happy with working mothers.'

'Oh, but Tara had twins,' the Archdeacon lost his calm again. He was defensive now.

'And I've got three children aged four and under!'

'Meg, I must urge you to see this parish and meet James. If you really don't want to, then of course that's your decision, but I must tell you that it may mean there is nothing else for you in this diocese.'

'What?' My moment of triumph evaporated, my hand reached for another twist of hair. I thought I heard Rosa stirring from a nap upstairs.

'We can't just go on making offers for you to turn down, Meg.' I could hear the smug smile in his voice.

'I hardly turned down the last one. I think...'

'Perhaps you should consider your future, Meg.' The conversation terminated abruptly.

Rosa began to wail.

All shall be well, I told myself over and over. Another parish, another diocese: March 1994 – standing in the cathedral, my children around me, another one due, ordained and offering peace.

The next morning I woke as a priest on Mothering Sunday, eager to celebrate Communion for the first time. When I arrived, the crumbling 1950s concrete church was bursting with daffodils. After two years of serving a disconsolate congregation of twenty, it was a shock to see so many people crowded into the uncomfortable pews.

As I stood to say the Prayer of Consecration over the bread and wine, the baby kicked hard, rippling my new purple chasuble. I spread my arms, a gesture of invitation and blessing. 'On the night that he was betrayed he gave thanks...'

Thanks and betrayal – odd companions, I mused. The baby kicked again. There would be no six-month maternity leave this time, but it was not a thought to entertain in the midst of my first 'Prayer of Thanksgiving'. I pushed the remembrance of the letter that had arrived a few weeks before ordination to the back of my mind.

> *"Although clergy are not employed and there is therefore*
> *no compunction on the diocese to make arrangements*
> *for maternity leave or pay, we have none the less decided*
> *to adopt a generous policy and to allow..."*

I had passed the letter over to Rob, unable to read on.

'You've been a deacon for six years and they hadn't even mentioned that you are not employed?' Rob held the letter like a viper and looked as white as if he had seen one. 'And they call this generosity?' Rob flung the letter onto the table. 'So now what?'

'Did you know that I can take eight weeks sick leave before I even need a doctor's note?'

'So?'

'So, ten days after a Caesarean section, do you think I will be fit to return to work?'

'Ah,' he hesitated, the light coming back into his eyes, 'I see.'

'Maternity leave till ten days after the birth, then sick leave and when that runs out I have all of this year's holiday saved up to take in one block. I'm also going to trade some time from before the birth – holiday cover. That gives me just over eighteen weeks, including their generous ten days, plus a week before the birth.'

'You've been thinking about this?' Rob grinned, reached over to cup his hands over mine.

'Endlessly.'

'This is my body...' I went on, coming back to the prayer, holding my hands cupped in consecration over the bread. In three weeks I would feed a baby with my own body and all would be well, it always was.

I was alone with the baby when the call came. The week-old Caesarean scar ached as I walked round and round the living room in an effort to comfort Silas. I struggled to hold onto the telophone, rocking as I strained to hear the Archdeacon, his tone formal, his words tumbling out fast to ensure no interruptions.

'I've had a chance to have a word about your next post, Meg. I think I should warn you that there are going to be no parishes becoming vacant. I really think that you must look to your own future. The bishop will, of course, be willing to release you.'

I put the phone down and buried my face in my quieted baby; released again.

The final release came seven years later.

The first assault became a media circus overnight. How brave I was to go straight back to work only two days after being held at knife point while the Church safe was robbed, the image of Silas seared into my inner vision throughout the attack. Surely a three-year-old wouldn't even remember me if I died now?

The second attack was ignored; I should forget it like everyone else. He was only a harmless schizophrenic, after all, his promises to take us both to God couldn't have been too terrifying and he'd only held me for half an hour while the police were called.

The third attack made me an embarrassment. I was wrong to

have informed the police, the hierarchy told me; it would only lead to bad publicity for the church.

Becoming ill after a series of assaults rendered me beyond forgiveness; how would such weakness look to the outside world?

'It is in the crucible of our own fallibility; in the patchwork of love and abuse that we somehow learn again that all will be well...' I had sermonised on that first Mothering Sunday after being ordained a priest.

Seven years later, I walked out of the service for All Souls knowing that something had changed forever. The vision of motherhood and ministry, one informing and enriching the other, was shattered, but my family were still there and waiting for me in the Vicarage; four children for whom the last few years had been clouded by living with an increasingly sick and broken mother.

I walked into my youngest child's room and held him tightly. I remembered the pristine promise of each baby, the immensity of love and hope that came with each birth. 'This is life in all its fullness,' I said aloud to the half-asleep child, 'You, not them.'

No more chasing parishes in a church that seemed only to be afraid of mothers and resentful of children. The choice was made and I knew that all would be well.

Eater of Ashes

Ally Thomas

Theirs was a highly combustible relationship. Not a slow, lingering burn, but instant. Light the blue touch-paper and stand well back. I could see the starbursts reflected in his eyes. Seventeen, and seeing someone else, but burning for her, incandescent as he described her, a tremble and a catch in his voice before they even dated.

She was sparky, capricious and very, very bright. He glowed in her presence, ignited, alive, fired as this fifteen-year-old consumed and was consumed with a lust that needed no accelerant. How could he not fall for her? My mother warned me when she met her that she would always be high maintenance, needing to be constantly tended. Their laughter rang round the walls of our home and the light fittings shook. The logs roared in the stove and rattled the fire irons and I worried that this man-boy of mine, once so determined to pursue the career of his dreams would become distracted; that his ambition would become but little puffs of smoke as he settled so young.

I needn't have worried. His A-levels and auditions passed well and he was on his way. Her exam results were outstanding, too. My mother had a series of devastating strokes. Sorrow and worry and care of my poor paralysed, speechless Mam was juggled with flat hunting, buying pots and pans, cutlery, linen to equip him for his study years. I had to turf them out of bed to hang curtains at the window when he moved into his flat. She was indignant.

They saw each other every weekend. I was glad he had company and that he seemed to be okay, but at Christmas he came home, and he was dulled. Everything was grey and cold as clinkers. My bright young spark was ashen with depression. He wouldn't go back to his digs. We struggled to understand, but everything about him was flattened, monotone. Then she arrived and he seemed to light up a little again, a solution was found – they would stay together with her family. He would be all right now. He'd missed company, needed conversation, needed her.

I moved my mother into sheltered accommodation. Leaving behind her old life and careworn possessions was hard, but now she was cosy, warm in a small place rather than shivering in the empty rooms in which she had brought up her brood. I wasn't sure if I was doing the right thing, but only that I had to look to her future.

In late April, as I dressed my mother, I had a phone call from away, greeting me wryly as "Nan". I could hardly reply. Hearing that word felt like catching a molten cannon ball and I remembered the observations of a favourite woman poet. When a baby girl is conceived it contains the ova that will form its future offspring, so there is my great-grand-daughter in embryo, too.

I knew then, for a short while, what it was like to be immortal, and a tremendous sense of all that was past, present and future swelled in me. As a family we cried and laughed together, called each other by our newly pronounced titles and vowed support.

He came home to us in the blistering summer. Arriving at seven in the morning he was obviously broken, his thoughts scrappy and disjointed. Our GP helped while I tried desperately to put him back together. She screamed and ranted. I was trying my best to make him go back and tried to tell her. I felt so desperately sorry for her, but he was charred, flaking even. He returned to her, dropped out of college, and looked for a job while she completed exams. Foolishly we searched the web for courses for him and erroneously helped him with his overdraft.

We bought the wrong pram and maternity things. Her resentment was like Mount Etna, continually bubbling, frequently erupting. But, we reasoned, she had given up smoking. He wanted them to get their own place and with his first wages he bought a Dyson cleaner.

Our grand-daughter was born in December and we were told not to hurry down to see her, as there were plenty of other people there already. My heart felt branded by these words – *Don't hurry down*. We couldn't do anything else. My mother was reluctant to let me go, becoming increasingly unsure of herself, needing me a little more each day. I can feel the weight of the baby in my arms, smell her charcoal hair.

I have photographs. Twenty of them. Clutching her in my arms, smiling at the camera, *smirking* at the camera. Proud Grandma, beautiful baby, beatific Mum. My grandmotherhood lasted just a few more weeks. We saw her only once more. I took my mother with us, but by now we were not allowed to see the child without being supervised. She seemed convinced that we planned on kidnapping the baby. We put on our bravest faces, our pathetic cooing subjected to their blazing scrutiny, but it was worth it just to plant the little smiler in my mother's lap. Her eyes filled with joy, as mine did.

My son sees his baby once a month. She lives far away, and will soon be two, but there'll be no party here. You see, inevitably she got the baby. Our son came back with his depression, his Dyson and an HP agreement for which we settled.

I cannot give my love to my grand-daughter except in secret. Secret savings for when she goes to college. Lovingly, lovingly, I knit little garments, cardigans and coats, things to wrap her in and whilst I knit, a strand of my hair is woven in.

Sometimes I see video clips of her on my son's phone. She is a ray of light in which I cannot bask. A jolly ember glowing only within the eyes of her dad. Maybe in time things will improve. Maybe when she's old enough to ask. Maybe she wears the little red coat. I think of all these things as I vacuum up the dust. My face is burning with salt as I'm telling you all this, but as a mother-outlaw, I can do nothing. Singed by their passion, now I get to eat the ashes.

The Photographs

Carolyn Lewis

It was after your nanna died that I found the photographs. They were lying underneath a pile of books. The edges had curled, but the images were unmarked. Five black and white pictures. I remember the day when they'd been taken. It had been late October, leaves were falling and you perched on low branches of the trees we found.

I'd taken you to the wood; we were going to have a treasure hunt and I'd dressed you warmly, putting on layers of clothing, wrapping you in hand-knitted jumpers. I wanted you to be warm, but I wanted you to look good, too. I wanted you to look happy, well cared-for.

You were anxious to do exactly what the photographer was asking of you. I'd explained that he was a real photographer, someone who got paid for taking photos. Not like me, who took endless photos of the three of you, charting your progress, then keeping the results muddled together in a cardboard box on a shelf in the dining room.

When your dad left, he left the three of you, and he also left the box of photographs. I never understood that – surely he'd need them? Without them he wouldn't be able to see your faces every day. He never saw these photos. He wasn't with us when they were taken. Alun was with us. You knew him. He'd been to our house, sat in our garden, pushing you in turns on the squeaking red swing.

He was your dad's friend. They'd gone to school together and they used to sit drinking and swapping memories. He'd stay long after you'd all gone to bed. He'd stay while I ploughed through the ironing, while I put your games kits together, folding Brownie uniforms, cleaning your shoes.

When he came to see us after your dad left, you saw the large bunch of flowers he held, each of you took the tube of Smarties he'd brought. At the time it seemed to me that you recognised he still came to the house. You appeared to accept that where once he was your dad's friend, now he was mine.

It had been his idea to take photos of you. 'Let me do it properly,' that's what he said. 'They're beautiful children. Let me take some good photos of them.'

You were all intrigued by the camera, the lens that moved around. You watched in silence as he set it up, your eyes following him as he moved between sun-dappled clearings, trying to get the best light. You were all silent, understanding perhaps that these photos were serious, not the usual disorganised ones I took of you.

Without being told, you grasped each other's hands. You stood in a line waiting for the usual command. *Smile*. But he didn't ask you to smile – he asked you to sit on an old branch near the base of a tree. You glanced at each other, bemused looks on your faces. For a while the click of the shutter was the only sound. You sat perfectly still as Alun moved around you.

Then he asked you to walk towards the camera and once more you held hands as you fanned out, walking towards him and me.

When, a few days later, he brought the photos to show us, I was struck by the fact that you'd been so still, your faces gazing back at me. You looked wonderful, the shine on your carefully brushed hair, the way the three of you looked, three parts of a sisterly whole.

I showed the photos to everyone. 'Look at my girls.' I showed them to your nanna and poppa, I saw the tears in my mother's eyes as she gazed at them. My boss teased me – was I sure these beautiful children were mine? Neighbours asked if Alun would take photos of their children, but he refused.

I know I meant to buy frames for the photographs. I'd thought of hanging them in the hall, where I could see them each time I entered or left the house. I didn't buy any frames and we moved from that house and the photos somehow got lost in the upheaval.

Alun and I struggled with a relationship. We hovered around the fact that I was a newly single woman. He came to the new house; we sat in the garden in the summer and in the winter months he sat on the mismatched chairs in the living room. He watched as you began tap classes, saw how you struggled with spelling tests and celebrated your birthdays with a home-made cake. I so wanted you to like him, for my sake.

He asked me out to dinner, to the theatre, but after a while he seemed unwilling to understand that I needed reliable babysitters and these were hard to find. 'Ask the woman at the end of the road.' Once he said he felt sure the three of you would be all right on your own. 'They're sensible kids.' Eventually I realised he was merely an observer, a bystander in your lives. He stopped coming round.

I hadn't thought of those photos for years.

You were ten, eight and six when the pictures were taken. Twenty-three years later I can still see the gloss on your hair. I remember knitting those warm sweaters you wore.

I remembered the sunlight filtering through the remaining leaves. I heard again the sound of our footsteps crunching over the multi-coloured woodland carpet. I still remember the sound of the camera as it clicked.

What I did not remember was the look on your faces. Why hadn't I seen it before?

In these sombre photographs, your eyes are questioning, your faces are solemn, there is no laughter. Your faces are close together as if you were protecting each other.

I've no idea how these photographs came to be hidden amongst my mother's effects. She loved the three of you, spoke always of her pride in you. Over the years she displayed your school photos, your graduation photos, the glorious wedding day photos. But these five photos were hidden.

I took the photos home, placing them on the passenger seat of my car, and as I left Cardiff my eyes flickered constantly to them. Once home, I put them on my desk, my hands shifting them around, for some reason trying to remember the order they were taken. When the tears came it was because I could see what I had done, what my mother had seen and I had missed.

Now I can see that your faces were haunted, you were confused and frightened. You held each other's hands as support and comfort. The comfort you should have got from me.

It had only been a short while since your dad left, a matter of months. I'd tried hard to soften the blow, to tell you that it would make no difference to our lives. Your dad would still see you, he'd still love you.

I'd always known that one of the reasons Alun came to see your dad was me. He'd made that clear a few years before. Part of me felt flattered. I'd be lying if I said anything else. I began to lie, telling my husband a long complicated story. That bit was fine – I did it smoothly. Telling you, my daughters, that Mummy was seeing an old friend, 'catching up on news', that tore at me. Still does.

'Who's your friend? Do we know her?' This from my daughters who filled the house with their friends. I told you that you didn't know her, she was a friend from school. You liked that, you laughed at the thought of your mum wearing a school uniform, sitting behind a desk.

My marriage was dull, static and I'd been relieved when your dad finally left. I thought I'd be a good single parent. I thought I'd cope very well. I thought you'd accept the fact that I'd met someone else. I got it so wrong.

I let you down. That's the simple truth. It's in these photographs. Your complete bewilderment. Your uneasiness at the situation you found yourselves in.

Now I know why my mum didn't display these photos, why she cried when she saw them for the first time. She could see what I could not.

I'm sorry.

Bittersweet Baby

Marie France Jennings

But for a handful of stragglers not sure whether they should abandon their empty glasses on the lawn or hope for more champagne, the garden had emptied out. From the kitchen I heard the water running over the dirty plates, and the hired help in a song whose refrain was all she remembered. I could not ask her to stop for that would have been to acknowledge that my sleep was only pretence, a physical lie pulsating beneath closed eyelids.

Sleep. I wanted to stay awake to better imagine it, soft and kind, deep and forgiving, a land where children stopped crying and where I could believe that my life would return, unharmed.

I must have dozed, for when I next opened my eyes shadows from the trees hung like a painting against the sitting room walls, and in the hall, mother-in-law was granting her guests recognition for a well-accomplished task, no doubt shaking their hands in a manner that matched the solidity of her voice. 'Thank you so much for coming,' she told them as they left, 'so lovely to see you.'

I can remember the warmth of her tone when John first brought me to her home, but that was before she began to harbour doubts as to my suitability as a wife and issue provider. On the first count she remained unsure, 'the French,' she sighed loud enough for me to hear, 'Lovely people of course, but so emotional,' and while a grandson had been hoped for, a girl would do. For now.

She was pleased, though. The family had rallied round, treading upon their initial irritation, for who had ever heard of a baby blessing, when a christening – which I refused – is a well-recognised form of God acknowledgment. One might not believe in the Almighty – and they did not – but it was just as well to pretend. And the family did claim a bishop.

I wish it had been different, that few people had come, that it had rained that day so that I could have shelved it away amongst the banal, the unimportant, but even now, three decades later, I know that's nonsense.

My breasts were heavy with heat and trapped milk. From upstairs came the sound of a growing wail.

'I think she needs feeding, my dear.' The words pretended to care, but I heard the wheels and cogs of criticism grind against each other. New her role might have been, but standing behind me there was a grandmother who wanted to be heard. 'Shall I bring her down to you?'

I stretched, as a disturbed sleeper should. 'Thank you, but it might be best if I go upstairs.'

'As you wish my dear, as you wish.'

Ten days had been long enough for us to learn our lines. Breast feeding was to be carried out in the isolation of my bedroom – mine because John, my husband, the new father, had retreated to the spare room where he slept undisturbed – for there was sensuality in the suckling of nipples, an act that once heralded pleasure. I trundled to the room above where the object of my task was waiting. 'Hello, darling,' I cooed at the staring infant, 'let's get you fed, shall we?'

It was pleasurable, it was companionable, it was exciting holding a being I had created, but if I could have undone time it was to the expectant stage that I would have returned, to those glowing weeks when I contemplated motherhood as fulfilment of a dream, before the sullen medic violated my body with the metal cannula, again and again, until his boots squelched in the water running away from my body, and the pain grew tighter and tighter and turned crimson behind my eyes.

Sophie began to cry.

Contemporary wisdom dictated that feeding should be on

demand. That meant I was no more than a commodity, expected to produce milk from breasts as swollen as the udders of a contemplating bovine. Yet while the idea remained disturbing there was comfort in knowing that the boundaries of what I could achieve were set by nature, and if I kept my mind downcast, if I forbade myself more than a glance at the future, if I... Eyes shut, I sang to the bundle in my arms 'Rock a baby...' swaying her gently, then I altered the tune, lilted a kinder lullaby from my childhood '*Fais dodo Colin mon petit frère...*' Time to release my breasts, the right one first, distended, ballooned, blood vessels mapping the soreness to a deep purple. I let it sag towards the face puffed up by the exertion of crying,

'Be gentle little one, please.' Not an order, more of a plea. There was no gentleness in her biting. 'What are you doing, eating me up?' I sat on the nursing chair, pulled the child away from me, ran my finger along her gums. I knew the colour, flesh pink, reassuring, innocent. Sophie whimpered, and I bent to kiss her sweet smelling head.

'Let's try again, darling.' She sniffled, instinct guided her back to the breast, and together we communed, my body was on offer, my womb tightened and my child suckled, and I returned to my lullaby.

Eyes closed I saw us dancing; there were daisies and butterflies, afternoon sun, a meadow, a river in which to drown time, a swing creaking as it carried its light burden higher and higher towards the blue canvas above and...I screamed at the pain. 'Stop it!'

I looked down. What I held no longer seemed human: a form that twisted its shape, a red gash of a mouth across the face, and it began to crawl over me, and...

'What's the matter?' Mother-in-law stood in the doorway, her arms and hands flapping on either side of her pinafore, covered with printed castles that seemed to undulate above her abdomen. 'Is she hurt?' For an instant, the way she marched into the room I thought she was going to slap me. I shifted my weight on the pink veloured chair, and pulled down the towel draped over my shoulder, offering no more than a view of my back to the Inquisitor.

'Sophie does not know her own strength that's all,' and I added that we were both fine, stressing the both, intent as I was on claiming recognition for my importance.

'I'll get you some tea, my dear and then you should have a rest, you are looking pale,' – and not displaying enough motherly savoir-faire – I heard what remained unsaid, but it was not her I needed to fight, it was this creature, this…Mother-in-law would think me mad if I told her.

'No, I'm fine, thank you.' I wanted to smile but pain pegged down my mouth.

I must have sounded convincing enough because she retreated, 'We'll have a cold supper in the dining room, unless…' she looked around, took in the disarray, 'unless you'd rather eat in here,' and closed the door behind her.

It was not until I heard the clicking of the catch that I dared to lower my gaze, slowly, for I feared that an abrupt gesture could rouse the creature and …but I saw pink cheeks where crumpled flesh had lain before and the creation of my mind, fraying.

A branch was tapping at the window, dusk shredded shadows across the garden below, a spider secreted its web by the fire place, and downstairs the phone rang: normality. Sophie grew heavy in my arms. They hurt. An ache crawled inside my skull. I thought of darkness, of a night free from stars, of veins of gold from which love can be drawn. I wanted to sleep. Not allowed. Not yet. Needed freedom to sleep. I was trapped.

Had Sophie looked at me with seeing eyes, what would she have made of the face leaning towards hers? Her lips sucked, like those of a toothless beggar. She was waiting.

I listened to her breathing, and stared at her feet not large enough yet to fill up the wrinkled flesh. A finger grabbed my thumb; I leaned forward offering myself, body and thoughts.

I know now that somewhere between pain and pleasure there exists a place only visited by mothers. But I didn't then. It was like standing in a kind of twilight where fear and longing did battle, and when I set out to walk across the new world undefined by either time or distance, I panicked, tried to run and found I couldn't.

A needle piercing pain made me gasp, and I bent my head forward. Red was not the colour I had expected to see, not that I had thought further than the milky shades of the food streaming from my body.

Splashed across the white towel spread over my child's body, it looked as if bloody dribbles were turning into small jagged stars, and I watched a red line define my thigh beneath the cotton skirt open to a fan crumpling at my feet. I even thought I could smell the blood, sweet, like new milk.

'Sophie!'

Now she lay on my bed. I must have thrown her there. I crouched to the floor. We stayed like that with expectation dancing in the air. Had I screamed mother-in-law would have rushed in to see what I had done.

'Sophie, please, Sophie.' I pleaded with her. On my knees now I inched my way towards my baby. 'Please,' I whispered, 'my darling, please don't hurt, I love you...' I begged again, 'please...'

I heard a scream, and then feet pounding the landing.

Doors slammed shut, voices called out, another scream slit the background of white noises the way a knife would cut through a cloth. I climbed towards a dark sky, and then everything turned white.My arms ached and I couldn't raise them. I was a body lying in a bed, so weighty I sagged into the mattress, so neglected I smelt my sweat, so tired I didn't want to move. A face bent over mine, a hand hovered over my closed lids. 'Let her sleep.' The breath reeked of peppermint.

I woke to the sound of a woman singing. It took another darkening of the sky behind the window facing my bed before I realised that like her, I was caged, that there were six of us in a ward, locked, my neighbour whispered to me through clenched teeth, 'for our safety because the world outside is insane'.

Until then, for all its massive red brick body and tentacular single storey structures, Whitchurch Hospital had only existed on the periphery of my consciousness, much as it still does that of the city. Before my incursion into mental illness I had driven past the buildings overshadowed by the threatening branches of centenarian oak trees but failed to imagine the inmates, the shuffling down the endless corridors, the smell of stale urine, the sobbing in the night, the grunting that filled in the gaps left behind by missing words, and the dead eyes at the windows.

'Nurse,' a woman called, 'get this patient cleaned up and dressed, doctor wants to see her.'

Dr Knight seemed nice enough. I remember his name because he wore a dark suit when I wanted him dressed in shining armour, and with a dragon slaying sword in his right hand. 'We'll have a talk,' he said and led me to a small room where chairs bled yellow foam, metal ashtrays overflowed with cigarette ends, and magazines advertised last year's Christmas gifts while we lived through a mid July heat wave.

We sat face to face. 'You don't mind,' he said pointing at half a dozen young men in white coats over baggy trousers. 'They're students,' he smiled, ' pretty harmless I can assure you!' I nodded. They clicked their biros ready. I was not allowed to say much. I was made to listen.

'Conflict between expectation and reality,' he explained, 'an acute case of post natal depression. Delusions. Quite common. Hallucinations.' He turned towards me, patted my hand. 'This patient should be fine in a few weeks.' He faced the psychiatrists to be: 'Suggested treatment gentlemen?'

'What about ECT,' proposed a red-head who'd been staring at me through thick lenses, and whose mouth twitched rabbit fashion.

'We'll try and avoid electric shock treatment. Medication should be enough.'

Dr Knight rested his hand on my shoulder, 'Don't worry,' he

said, 'we'll look after you.'

They were happy. They had a name for what had happened to me. I just had me. And my baby. John brought her in a few days later. I talked to her. She looked so sweet; she gurgled her funny sounds, reached towards the plastic animals stretched over her pram, and dribbled a little milk on the head of a bunny rabbit embroidered pink on her white knitted jacket. I was not allowed to hold her. Not yet. Too soon, too dangerous. For her or for me, John didn't say. He didn't have to.

She was good at imitating the smiles poured over her by the nurses, and I liked to watch her hands dance in the air, and the way her eyelashes rested like tiny blond petals on the edge of her cheeks.

I couldn't afford to weep. The moment strong emotions crawled out of my mind, the moment they looked out of my eyes, they got drowned in chemical strawberry syrup laced with medication. I had come to recognise the bitterness behind the sickly sweet taste, like John's anger hidden behind the mundane words.

He was relieved when the bell rang the end of visiting time. He deposited a kiss on my forehead, – no more than a friend would – and told me not to worry, that he was coping fine. Which of course was true because he had moved back home to mother, and she had taken over my child, the daughter she'd never had.

I was in the art room when John came back later that day. Alone this time.

He walked to the drinks machine and I heard the coins drop down the metal chute.

'I have accepted a three year lectureship in Brisbane,' he said, his back to me, 'and I wanted to tell you what I decided to do about Sophie.' He took a sip of coffee

I waited.

'I won't be taking her with me.' He stared at a small archipelago of brown stains on the carpet. 'My parents will look after her. I'll see her during the summer holidays, and of course we will arrange for you to visit when we feel you are ready.'

'I'll be better soon,' I told him, and thought he might have reached out for my hand.

'It's too early to tell,' he said, adding that my first priority had to be with my daughter.

'Fine,' I said, 'fine.' I knew it wasn't what I wanted to say, but my brain had grown slower; it wouldn't let me organise my thoughts. I could climb the first flight of an idea and then where the landing should have been, nothing but space and ideas floating in the air and no butterfly net to catch them with. I struggled for words. I knew they were there. Like I knew John had turned stranger, but that I didn't want to lose Sophie and couldn't articulate my fears.

That night I was sipping hot milk in front of a blurry television screen in the day room, when, screaming for Jesus, one of the new patients ran through the window and landed in the garden below. Glass everywhere. Prickly heat on my forehead.

Warm trails down my cheeks. Hands to support me, the smell of disinfectant, my body stretched out on a hard surface, and a sun strong light that had me blink salt and tears down the opened slivers of flesh. You can't see the scars now. Not unless you know where to look.

Maybe it was the shock of seeing the man lying in the wet grass and the blood pooling by his head, may be, when they tore through my skin the shards of glass pierced deeper than physical pain, reached my subconscious, and traced a narrow path to sanity. I can't be sure, but I think that was the day I turned round and began the slow walk back to the pre-birth me; measured steps at first, silent steps, because it is not easy to walk away from the crouching tiger that is madness. It took time to convince the psychiatrists and my marriage didn't survive. But I won the legal battle, the judge declared me sane, and I made it to Sophie's birthday; I held my daughter close, and helped her blow out the fat candle planted deep on a clumsy sponge cake smothered with pink icing sugar.

Starting Out

Fiona Collins

Our son was born on Anglesey, Ynys Môn, in the depths of winter, over thirty years ago. In chronological time it happened a long time ago: nearly half my life has passed, all of his. But every year, at the beginning of December, when his birthday comes around, it seems as though no time has elapsed at all, as if the event recurs every year, in some pattern of cyclical time triggered by the season, and by memory.

In the autumn of 1973 we had moved into a farmhouse which had not been used for over a dozen years, except as an occasional holiday home by a city family, until we arrived. It was a struggle to turn the cold house back into a home, a place where a baby could be raised: cosseting and encouraging an ancient Rayburn, coaxing the plumbing system to pump spring water up from the well in the field, lugging every bag of supplies through the mud bath created around the house by a nosy herd of dozy, shaggy bullocks.

We had no phone in the house, and mobile phones were yet to be invented, incredible though that now seems. The way to make a phone call was to fill a pocket with change, wrap up warmly, squelch through the bullocks' mud, follow the pitted drive to the gate (about quarter of a mile in itself), then climb the steep lane to the lake, and trudge along the shore for the best part of another mile to a lay-by, where there was a public phone box. It was not a system guaranteed to bring quick results. Full of the blithe confidence of youth, I was not at all worried about going into labour in such a remote setting. In fact I lamented the refusal of the local midwives to manage a home birth for me, in spite of my requests. Instead I had been booked into the nearest general hospital, which was then St David's in Bangor, this being some while before Ysbyty Gwynedd was built in its place.

The baby was due towards the end of December – being young and fairly disorganised I wasn't very sure of "my dates" – and as autumn turned to winter my unwilling pilgrimages to the antenatal clinic in Holyhead were increased from monthly to weekly excursions. To check the readiness of the baby to join the rest of us in the big wide world, I was required after one appointment to provide, not just a sample of urine, but the product of an entire day's emissions. Arriving at the next week's clinic with the huge, swashing bell jar with which I had been furnished for this task, I felt incredibly embarrassed by this copious evidence of my inner workings. The doctor did the tests on the bell jar, and on me, and sent me home with the observation: 'The baby's a better size now. Come back next week and your delivery should occur soon after that.'

That same night I went into labour, assisted, so I've always believed, by the two cream cakes I ate with my neighbour as I reported back to her on my clinic visit.

I woke in the early hours of the morning feeling distinctly odd, with contractions going on. I'd been having Braxton-Hicks contractions for the best part of a fortnight, usually at night, and the doctor's authoritative words had convinced me that the baby would not come until Christmas. It was only the sixth of December. However, the baby clearly did not agree with the doctor's opinion. He was on his way. I didn't realise this as I padded softly to and from the toilet, not wanting to wake my partner Rob. I thought it was just "another rehearsal". Eventually I gave up altogether on going back to bed, dressed as quietly as I could, in the baggy jumper and home made corduroy maternity trousers I had been wearing day in, day out for the last few weeks, and crept downstairs to the warmth of the kitchen. Rob slept soundly through all this.

In the downstairs loo I was sick a couple of times, which I put down to my greed with the cakes. It was only when, a little after six o'clock, as I sat on the toilet for the umpteenth time, and my waters broke with a strange deep popping sound, that I realised this was the real thing. I called up to Rob from my perch on the toilet, not daring to get up while the water gushed from me. He was still deeply asleep. I shouted again and again. And again. At last his pale, startled face appeared in the open doorway of the toilet.

'I think you'd better phone for the ambulance,' I said.

He began to flap around like a cross between a mother hen and a headless chicken. After helping me to emerge rather gingerly from my self-imposed exile in the toilet, he struggled into his clothes and started off on the route march to the phone. It took him about twenty minutes to reach the phone box, and make his breathless call. Then the ambulance had to come the twenty-odd miles from Bangor. Then they had to find the place, and negotiate the ill-made drive, the bullocks, and the mud.

The ambulance finally arrived a little after eight o'clock, at about the same time as the watery winter sun was pushing up into the morning sky.

Rob had acquiesced, with some relief, to the hospital switchboard operator's suggestion that a midwife accompany the ambulance. She picked her way fastidiously through the mud to the door, followed by two chirpy ambulance men. Rob let them in. I was lying on the floor of the living room having contractions, as this was one of the few comfortable options I had been able to find. By this time I was completely focussed on what was happening inside my body, and quite detached from the outside world. My choice of position seemed to scandalise the midwife, who wanted me tidily off the floor and into the ambulance. If she had only stopped to examine me then, she could have delivered Sam on the living room carpet.

Instead we had a rather frantic scramble out of the house and into the ambulance. The midwife said I must not walk, as my waters had broken, and in spite of my protests that I was fine to walk, indeed I preferred to walk, the two ambulance men linked hands and made a seat to carry me over the mud to their waiting vehicle. I remember that carry: my arms around their shoulders, their hot earnest faces close to mine, their muttered directions to each other as they tried to negotiate the mud. The midwife bustled behind, and Rob brought up the rear. It was only just getting light, a still cold December morning.

We made it to the ambulance, and all bundled in: the two ambulance men in the front, Rob squashed in with the midwife and me in the back. We started to bump down the track to the gate. The midwife, once more in her own element, at last got me to wriggle out of my faded cords and overstretched pants, so she could examine me. The ambulance reached the lane and whined up the hill in first gear. Once the lake came into view the driver turned right, towards the main road, to take us to Bangor.

'No. No. Stop here. Stop a minute,' the midwife called out sharply. The driver pulled over into a lay-by, in front of the little row of cottages which line the ridge. Through the back window of the ambulance, over my domed belly, I could see across the flat landscape of Môn towards Holy Island. Below the dark clouds overhanging the horizon, the winter dawn streaked the sky silver, lemon, palest green.

'Push now, push,' ordered the midwife peremptorily. I pushed. Once, twice, once more: gritting my teeth, screwing up my face, putting all the strength I could find behind the irresistible commands of my body, in comparison with which the midwife's commands were pathetic little squeaks.

The baby's head appeared between my thighs. I pushed again, still aware of that broad horizon, that pale dawn: metaphor for the new life there between my upraised knees. My baby. He was long and thin: his face still, almost serene, his hands huge, fingers spread wide. He weighed 6lb 4oz: not bad for a little fellow who was three or four weeks earlier than expected.

The ambulance men called out cheerily to Rob, their hearty

male voices cutting across the midwife's words of instruction. They leaned over the back of the driver's seat, pumped Rob's hand in congratulation. They had never had a birth in their ambulance before, they told him. The three of them were as pleased as if they'd organised the whole thing themselves. Rob, the new father, had never had a birth at all. He was almost dancing on the spot, jigging up and down in excitement.

The midwife, exasperated, was trying to bring this jolly crowd's attention back to the matter in hand. She called out sharply to the drivers. They hushed, looked towards her.

'Not much point in going all the way to St David's now,' she told them. 'We'll take them to the Gors instead.'

And so we set out for the little maternity hospital at Holyhead, where only second and subsequent, uncomplicated births were scheduled, for there was no obstetrician on the premises. She gave me an injection – I never found out what it was. She said it was to hold back the placenta, so they could deliver it at the Gors. Which they duly did.

The cord was cut, and my baby was wrapped in an ambulance blanket. The midwife gave him to me. The driver drew slowly, gently, out of the lay-by and set off sedately down the lane, to take us as smoothly as he could on the rest of the journey. I held my baby in my arms as tenderly as I could, and talked softly to him, all the way to Holyhead. Our first journey together: my son, his father and I. When we set out we were two. Now we were three. A family.

It was a little before nine in the morning, on 6th December 1973. For our son, for Sam, his life journey was just beginning, beginning with this actual journey into the west: towards the sea, the winter morning, the start of a new day.

Dancing on the Railway Line

Dorothy Gilroy

I walked out of St David's Hospital, Bangor, leaving my baby behind. She was in the Special Care Baby Unit. The consultant's words had eaten into me like poison. 'This is a child who might never walk or talk; they have smaller heads, thick sloppy tongues, poor muscle tone.' It was 1973; I had never heard of Down's Syndrome, so he had said 'mongoloid', usually born to older mothers – I was only 32. 'It'll affect the whole of your family life,' he added.

I thought of my other two children, Duncan – five and Trish – three. My mum had died not long after Trish was born, my father only a month before I had the baby. 'Baby?' I had barely glanced at her. One of my friends went and looked at her flat face, slanty eyes, tongue drooling and said, 'Do forget her.' We called her Rachel, registering a child we had never seen and hoping that someone would conveniently dispose of it for us.

She was taken into care in Holyhead. I sat in a stupor. The odd neighbour called in, but people didn't know what to say. My husband was in the RAF and the Group Captain's wife came with flowers and well-meaning platitudes. My best friend came from the north and we sat on Llanddwyn Beach watching another family of three children playing in the sand and I turned to my friend and said, 'We'll never be able to do things like this.' The following day the mother of another Down's child called. She was jaded, haggard, worn out. 'I'm lucky,' she said. 'Our nan helps me a lot and we all go to Butlins. They have child minders there.' Butlins? We were an outdoor family, liked walking, swimming, camping and we had no local family support.

The social workers started to call. Gentle persuasion started our lives. 'Come and see her.' We went and "it" was ~~and~~-faced, slanty eyes, small head, asleep on her back, ~~~~ my son leaned over the cot and stroked her cheek. I wouldn't go again. I knew what they were trying to do.

It was 1973. Words such as "mongoloid" and "idiot" were used openly. There was a high death rate for these kids – their small chests and short throats encouraged chest infections. 'Perhaps she'll die,' I thought.

Then one day in June another Down's mum arrived. 'Come with me to Llangefni! Come and see the school.' School? No one had mentioned anything outside the baby, the cot and why I wouldn't hold her. But there was a new school, there was a teacher and kids playing out in the sun, clumsy kids, lame kids, dribbling kids, lopsided kids, but they were doing things and this mum said, 'For God's sake, life is what you make it. No one is perfect in this world.'

The social workers came again and they persuaded us to have her home for the weekend. Some neighbours crossed the road when they saw me with the pram. I retreated into the house and brooded. My husband went and climbed a mountain. My GP called by and said, 'They're often no real problem, sit her in a corner and play music.' I imagined a drooling, slanty-eyed blob: who was going to look after this? I wanted to work.

What was the turning point? The school, the kids' reaction, a Quaker aunt and uncle who had looked at Social Services support and said, 'Be flexible.' And the fact that she seemed like a 'normal baby' but much slower in development.

So gradually with longer and longer stays, Rachel became part of our lives and we took her permanently in October 1973 when she was six months old. It was isolating. I felt embarrassed taking her out. As she developed so, so slowly I used to lie about her age. I was too embarrassed to ask friends to have her and most of them had "normal" toddlers to deal with. But Duncan and Trish loved her and played with her and Duncan fed her sometimes – it took so long for her to suckle that I would prop him up in a big chair with his bottle arm supported.

I remember going to a party. I often didn't elaborate on the family but I recall telling someone I had three children, the youngest of whom was "mentally handicapped" and his response was, 'Goodness! You don't look like a mother of a handicapped child!' Those words stayed with me and I think from then onwards I was determined to prove I was as "normal" as anyone else. I found a child minder for Rachel after a huge search and went back to teaching part-time.

But my husband? Rachel had inevitably placed restrictions on our life and his career seemed to be at a standstill. I hadn't realised his growing restlessness, which culminated in his leaving the RAF and joining British Airways, commuting from Anglesey on to long haul flights. I was, therefore, busier than ever when he was away "doing the routes". Rachel was often ill with chest complaints and juggling jobs, kids and support for her was exhausting, so that he often came home jet-lagged to a fairly stressed-out household.

And then he met an air hostess. I came home unexpectedly from work one lunch time to find him sitting at the kitchen table looking at a photograph of a raven-haired beauty at least ten years younger than me. There ensued months of hell – he'd given her up, he said, but he hadn't. He was on a trip, he said – but he had gone to Rome with her. He left and came back, but used to sneak out to make phone calls to London. It couldn't go on. He finally left our house at five one morning in July, right at the start of the summer holidays. I stood in desolation and watched him drive off in a loaded car to be with her. He went to live with his air hostess in Surrey and we were now a single parent family.

Looking back I have often wondered whether this had more effect on Rachel than I realised. I put a huge effort that summer into keeping Duncan and Trish happy and stable, trying to do as much as we could together. I found a small care home to give us a break from Ray for two weeks, but wonder in retrospect how much she suffered from the seemingly inexplicable disappearance of her father and then being left in a home for two weeks. Be that as it may, Rachel was now six and that was the start of the Wild Years.

Down's people placid? Down's people easygoing? Not our Rachel: toddler, remedial, adolescent, all rolled into one and certainly showing signs of spirit and intelligence.

Not long before her father left, there had been an open day at RAF Valley. Officers and "wives" were allocated places in a select enclosure with front-line view of the display. We went as a family, well-dressed with warnings about good behaviour. The Group Captain was there to receive us and before we could stop her, Rachel pushed through the reception line, stood sturdily in front of him, thumbs in the air, pronouncing loudly, 'Hiya! Rock on Tommy!' Luckily he had a sense of humour.

She seemed perpetually restless. During her first day at school, they watched her play with a pencil sharpener, knock it off a table, scramble down after it, push it along the floor and then crawl off down a corridor – her first escape bid! I had always kept a very tight rein on her as had the child minder and it seemed that, away from us, her mind was set on doing what *she* wanted, when *she* wanted, and could not, would not, listen to reason. She was hell-bent on running away, just slipping, slithering, sidling away. In Marks and Spencer one crowded Christmas time, Rachel disappeared down packed escalators, off to Chester's city walls. On trips to Bangor she would duck under shop counters and run down the pedestrianised High Street. She learnt bad language from her peer group and used it indiscriminately. Her closest friends at school were both Down's, but gentle, calm and rather placid. Rachel was sparky but so naughty.

When she was six she became a member of a local Gateway Club, a Special Needs Youth Group, well staffed with student helpers. I went to pick her up one night and she was in the front lobby of a large mansion where it was held, a sturdy wee soul waving her hands flat across her chest. 'No come in! Go home!'

'What's happened?'

'No come in!'

I went into the main room. There was a police woman sitting there and a throbbing silence. There were tropical greenhouses by the old hall and they had taken the Gateway members to look at some plants and butterflies. Rachel had "escaped" and got onto the main London-Holyhead railway line, climbing through a small hole in the large protective fence. A member of the public had spotted her from the main road above the high cutting and dialled 999. She was happily dancing and jumping from sleeper to sleeper with no sense of fear or danger.

Two weeks later at the same Gateway Club they had a magician. He was about to do a rabbit trick when Rachel popped up behind him – she had slipped off a chair and crawled round. 'Rabbit's here!' she shouted, completely ruining his trick.

As a break Rachel was offered Sunday visits with a local family. She had two: on the first she had a fight with kids in the road, injuring one with a stone, and on the second one, she climbed a slide and wouldn't come down, hanging precariously over the edge and laughing with glee, taunting the scared family below.

Rachel was not always naughty, but the odds on bad behaviour were high. It meant it was difficult to leave her with other people. She had a habit of lying down in the street if she didn't want to go somewhere or do something, or tugging at you to get where she wanted to go. You had to be careful – smacking was allowed in those days, but you would not want to he seen hitting a person with learning difficulties and having poor skin tone, she marked easily. I was warned by the school when after a "naughty breakfast" she arrived with a hand mark on her bottom.

There was one particularly bad episode when her teacher was ill and Rachel gave the supply teacher a really bad time. Even her less able classmates were full of the stories of her throwing her books and pencils around the room. Around the same time an elderly aunt and uncle came to stay and had a real scare with her in Beaumaris. They were buying her ice cream when she broke away from them and sprinted down the pier, luckily to be caught by a fisherman as she hurtled towards the end.

But how to get this girl to behave? Everywhere she went there were bad reports – I couldn't trust her with anyone else. Stubborn? She would lie on the pavement and refuse to budge. She would grab sweets in shops. She had to be held in a vice or away she would go.

It was decided to call in a psychologist and we had a group meeting. There were two outcomes. One was that for a Down's, Rachel was reasonably intelligent, as evidenced even by her slithering escape tactics, and we needed to build on that. The other was that both her teacher and myself were fairly strong and controlling. She respected our control most of the time but then played up anyone who didn't have that control. I was assigned a community nurse who tracked Ray and myself and it was agreed first to move her into an ESN (moderate) Unit instead of the ESN (severe) Unit she was in. It was also agreed that I should try to "let go" and normalise her. She was enrolled into the local guides despite the trepidation of one or two mothers. Guides found her quite difficult and some of the parents felt she was too disruptive. We managed to find a volunteer who went with her and was such a wonderful help. She also joined the Woodcraft Folk – a kind of left-wing green, almost "anti-guide" group, and seemed very happy in the more laid back atmosphere. This was still back in the eighties – nowadays Down's people are seen in many special interest groups, in mainstream schools and holding down full-time jobs.

Rachel soon learnt to read, which has been such a bonus. She loves the soaps and gets the various soap magazines. She doesn't read books, but used to love having stories read aloud. She learnt to write simple letters and read and understand a bus timetable. Unfortunately, still being in a specialised unit, she was subject to some bullying and came home several times asking what a 'mong' was. She was also offered a one-day-a-week placement in the local village school. In the open plan setting she lasted just three weeks. The first week she climbed a ladder to join a slater on the roof. The second week she strolled out and walked home. She wouldn't sit quietly with the children, and she was sent back to the special school.

We lived in a small cul-de-sac where there were quite a few young children, and I told the mothers I was trying to get her out to play. It wasn't worth it – her first time out she swung on an up-and-over garage door and a child ended up in A & E. She wouldn't stay with the kids on the road – there would be a knock on the door, yet again the cry 'Rachel's run away!' and off we would go. During one scare she was found upstairs in a neighbour's bathroom, about to climb into a full bath she had run!

A major bonus in Ray's life is that she loves water, and has become an excellent swimmer. We used to go to the beach a lot and she would crawl fearlessly into the sea. So much for that early day on Llanddwyn Beach! I was once gossiping with the same friend on the shore of a lake in Cumbria when we looked up and there was Rachel bobbing about happily in a Woolworth's rubber ring, way way out on the lake with cruisers and speedboats.

Through school she was selected for the Special Games and became extremely competitive, particularly in swimming. But again, the strop. She had done well in the junior band, got gold and silver medals but was streamed by age into an older band at the age of fourteen. She didn't win any medals. When presented with a "well done" small cup by a lady mayoress in front of the many people there, she used "unsavoury language" and dramatically cast the cup into the swimming pool. She was returned to me off the bus in disgrace.

At eighteen Rachel joined a course at the local Technical College where I worked. Her course had an annual trip, usually to a city. Rachel had gone off to York this year and I was having my coffee break when someone came in and said, 'There's been hassle on the Special Needs trip to York.' My heart sank. Rachel had wandered away from the group in a large superstore – didn't like looking at fabrics, so went to the music centre instead. Headphones on and into a sound booth. She ended up in the police station and half the group missed out on a theatre trip. On the second year of her course, they were going to Edinburgh and Rachel's tutor warned me she was going to watch Rachel everywhere on this trip. ('Even if it means handcuffs, Dorothy!') It was near Christmas and Rachel had been wanting a black strappy dress for Christmas parties. Well, they had three days around Edinburgh, in small groups, with Rachel well under control, and had all convened to end the trip in the Waverley Centre, a circular central shopping mall off Prince's Street. Rachel's tutor did a head count (letting go of Rachel) – and off she went! She was found twenty minutes later in a very posh dress shop, trying on a cocktail dress worth £250, watched by bemused assistants.

Rachel is now thirty-three. She lives in a small group home in Anglesey, holds down a full-time job in a market garden, travels on buses on her own and uses a mobile. She still has her dramatic moments, can strop and sulk, can over-enjoy her alcohol, but is now a generally likeable young woman who leads a full life, as do many people with Down's Syndrome these days. The Wild Years seem behind us.

And one more story – for her thirtieth birthday present I took her to London for a touristy weekend. We rode the open-top bus circuit, went on the river and then to see "Mamma Mia". On the Sunday (having watched Diana's funeral in 1997) she wanted to see Westminster Abbey. It was April 2003 and Tony Blair had announced Britain was going into Iraq. Parliament Square was full of protesters with whom I greatly sympathised. We stopped and chatted to them, then at Rachel's request went on to look at Number Ten Downing Street. Rachel marched straight up to a young policeman outside the wrought-iron gates and announced, 'We've come to shoot Tony Blair!' A look of absolute horror crossed his face and he fingered down to his gun holster. Was this a clever decoy? I dragged Rachel away in embarrassment. Oh, Rachel, smart enough to bad-mouth Tony Blair, daft enough to threaten us with a security alert. What a girl!

Early Learning

Joy Tucker

I learned many lessons from my dolls. They were kept in the toy cupboard underneath the living-room window and I think I played with them most days. I know I had a routine in the way I set them out. If asked to recall my earliest memory, there would be a flash photograph of my dolls, in full colour and intricate detail, instantly printed on my mind, each doll in its set position. And if pressed to speak of that particular occasion on which I remember playing with them, there would be, even now, a strange mixture of pain and pleasure in the tone of my voice, like a sad chorus in a happy song. Or perhaps I would try to deny my own memory.

On the day I remember, the newest doll in my collection was Maureen, who wore a blue dress and had bright yellow hair, which had been combed too many times since Christmas. The oldest doll was Sonny Boy, handed on to me from my sister when she decided she was too old to play with dolls any more. Sonny Boy had lost a foot and his face was a little battered, but he still looked quite smart and could sit on the wide windowsill beside Maureen when the game was playing at schools.

My sister had been going to school for a while then, and must have told me what happened there, showing me how to make the dolls sit up straighter and look at the blackboard and how to raise an arm when they wanted to say something to me, their teacher. There were a couple of rag-dolls, too, Betsy and Mabel, who never sat up straight enough. And then there was Cherry-Ripe, my favourite. Cherry-Ripe was a baby doll, fat and smiling, with rosy dimpled cheeks and blue eyes, which could close under long curling lashes, and she said "Ma-ma" when you turned her over.

I loved playing with Cherry-Ripe. I learned how to wrap her in a shawl, sing to her, rock her to sleep, to be her mother. Her special place was in a small wooden cradle with a patchwork quilt, where she would lie very still with her eyes closed until it was time to get her up and washed and dressed.

But on this particular day, the day of my earliest memory, I was not playing with the dolls. It was a strange day. My sister was not at school, and she had been crying. My father was not at work, and had taken my sister out somewhere. Before they left, he looked as if he too had been crying. They said they wouldn't be long, and no one would tell me what was wrong.

I knew my mother wasn't feeling very well. And that morning the house had been full of people coming and going, the doctor, two district nurses. Later on it became very quiet. I had watched from the window as first the doctor and then the nurses left. 'You play with your dolls,' Annie had said, hurriedly opening the toy cupboard and tumbling the dolls out in a bundle. 'Be a good girl now. Stay in here. I'm going to sit with your mother. You must stay here till your father gets back.'

I didn't like Annie, who came in sometimes to look after us when my mother wasn't well. I didn't like the way she mashed potatoes, leaving lumps. And if a button came off, Annie would say she didn't have time to sew on buttons, and stuck a safety-pin where the button should be. And the safety-pin had to stay there until my mother was better again. That day Annie had even put the dolls in the wrong places. Betsy was in the cradle, Sonny Boy was lying on the window-sill, the others on the floor. My mother always knew the right places for the dolls, just as she knew how to get lumps out of mashed potatoes and to sew on buttons in a minute. I can remember wishing that my mother would be better soon.

It was too quiet to play with the dolls, but I knew they'd be happier in their correct places. Then, when I had sorted them out, combing Maureen's hair, putting socks on Sonny Boy, and placing Cherry-Ripe safely back under the patchwork quilt in the cradle, I decided I might as well play for a while, and went to get a face-cloth from the bathroom, to wipe their faces. I tiptoed past my mother's bedroom, so that Annie wouldn't hear, and closed the bathroom door behind me.

There was a wooden tray across one end of the bath where soap, flannels and nailbrushes were kept. Instead, it was covered with a white cloth and on top of the cloth was a baby. At first I thought it was a new doll. It was the same size as Cherry-Ripe and it lay as straight and still, with its eyes closed under a fluff of eyelashes. But Cherry-Ripe was pink all over when her clothes were taken off. This doll was a colour I had not seen before – a sort of bluish-white. I stood for a long time looking, then I touched its skin. It was soft, but very cold. I waited, hoping the baby would open its eyes and have a smiling face, but somehow I knew it would not.

Very quietly I opened the bathroom door. I could hear a murmur of voices from my mother's room. Annie and my mother were talking. Swiftly I ran to the living-room, to my dear doll family and took the patchwork quilt from Cherry-Ripe's cradle. And then in the bathroom, where the baby lay as still and cold as ever, I placed the quilt over the little dead body, and ran back to play with my dolls.

The episode was not mentioned until many years later, at a time when I was hoping to start a family. I told my mother about what I had seen on that long-ago day of the dolls. Even then there were not many words to say. We both cried a little – for each other, I think, and perhaps for the hopes and the fears of all mothers.

Up With The Birds

Hilary Lloyd

I recall exactly where I was when he told me: leaning back against our Rayburn with the oven door open to warm my bum, eager for our weekly chat over the phone; the one that soothed my problem-ridden life for a few precious moments. Afterwards, I had no other problem but his.

'I've seen a consultant today, Mum,' he said in a calm and reasonable voice. 'And he says I've got ME, but you're not to worry.'

Not to worry? I froze, couldn't find a single word, not even one of sympathy or encouragement, not the tiniest little 'there-there, it'll be all right, just you see' and a sticking-plaster to make it better.

I listened to his plans for recovery. He'd researched it all thoroughly before telling me he knew of several alternative practitioners who could cure him inside a year.

A year? I knew better than most that it would take a whacking great chunk out of his young life, just when his career was developing, just when he'd found the perfect woman to share his life. Just when they'd bought a tiny house to live in together for ever and a day and a few extra if their love had anything to do with it. I knew because the friend I lived with had already stumbled through three years of the same bloody affliction and showed little sign of recovering for a long time yet. And I knew because of what I'd researched during stolen hours online, secret times my friend knew nothing of, because she too refused to acknowledge the awful truth, yet hated the thought of me losing hope too.

'I *will* get better soon, Mum,' my son said. 'I'm not like

everyone else.'

Such charming logic. True in a sense. It's a mother's prerogative to say her son is a one-off, not only in her eyes, but in those of his friends, colleagues, girlfriend. She once confided in me that he was so special she wanted to know how I'd done it so she could do the same when they had children. How I'd done it? All I did was give him life, bring him up, stick plasters on his knees and rescue him from hazards he'd leapt into without a thought beyond the thrill of the moment. All I did was bring him up mostly on my own, teach him to try different foods before deciding he didn't like something. All I did was spend time with him, hours counting flowers in the park or busy at the kitchen table helping him make castles and fire engines out of cereal packets and Lego. Don't all mothers? When he was ten, I taught him how to use a washing machine. To my mind it isn't hard to stuff clothes in, turn a dial and press the ON button. If everything comes out grey or pink then it's obviously time to suss the scientific aspects of washing clothes, and he did, eventually.

I also squeezed him through the hard times and laughed with him through the good ones. I endured his teens and relished his twenties when he turned round and accepted my needs and foibles and tantrums instead of groaning about them.

And in his late twenties I spent a fortune I didn't have on the last single room in London, no more than a crappy cupboard in some poncy hotel, so that I could attend his first night, which of course he'd forgotten to mention until the last minute. I sat in the stalls and gaped at the extent of his wonderful, wonderful talent before applauding so loudly he would have died of shame in his teens. Then I went back to the hotel, drank most of a bottle of celebratory wine I'd smuggled into my room and wept buckets of maternal pride.

And then at thirty he was struck down. A melodramatic phrase, of course, but what other words could describe how I felt when he told me. I knew everything there was to know about ME. I'd lived alongside its effects for too long. I'd survived periods of hope so quickly smashed to the floor. I'd picked myself up, found a lower gear and ploughed on, managing my friend's despair with cheerful stoicism, turning ever more practical so she didn't have to worry that our rural plot would fall into ruins without her skills. I learned not to show my exhaustion from all the extra work so she wouldn't feel guilty. I learned how to cut grass, slay weeds, lop shrubs and grew to love the peace of outside work when birds cried and swooped just for me to marvel at their song and their aerobatics. I learned to love the deafening roar of our ill-tuned mower – it cut me off from the sodding world and its problems – and even grew to like starting it, surviving the heart attack-inducing rage when it refused to obey me. Kicking the rusting heap into life meant I'd end up back in the house vented of all anger and with a smile on my face instead of a scowl of self-pity about the injustices ladled into my life.

So when my son told me he too had ME I knew all the things he couldn't even start to imagine. I'd seen them all. I knew that his initial determination to get better quickly would soon drown in despair. I knew that no amount of vitamins and acupuncturist's needles and homeopathic magic potions would make any lasting difference. I knew that occupational therapy and physiotherapy, even psychotherapy, would not help one jot. I knew the intimate details of every macrobiotic diet plan or regime of graded exercises, and I knew he'd have days when he couldn't summon the will, never mind the physical energy, to get himself out of bed.

I also knew ME would end his career. And it did. In its first year, he tried to carry on, bless him, by taking on small jobs, only to find they made him more ill. I sympathised and coaxed him out of his black moods. I spent hours on the phone giving him verbal hugs and sticking plasters. I wrote him long newsy emails and letters, carefully skirting my physical prowess in the garden and concentrating on what I'd seen and heard in the great outdoors. I resisted the instinct to rush to his side and nurse him as I had done in his infancy and, cruellest of all, I had to stop going to see him because he couldn't cope with visitors, not even his mother.

One of the side effects of ME, after the initial exhausted state eases, is that patients look and behave normally in the presence of others. They want so desperately to be better that they'll dig down for their last scrap of stamina to appear so. Afterwards they collapse, sometimes literally and sometimes for weeks. So I ran up a phone bill instead, the only way to cover the two hundred and fifty miles between us, and I jacked up my emotions and my voice whenever I spoke to him.

ME also meant the end of his beautiful relationship. Oh, how I cried when he told me she was leaving. And oh, how I raged at her, silently, of course – wasn't I an expert by then at keeping my fury firmly cooped up? But why couldn't she stay the course, she who'd told me he was everything to her? Love conquers all, the saying goes. It survives the storms and sulks. It endures illness and financial problems. No glitch is too much for the head-down, shoulders-against-the-wheel attitude that two people share if they love each other.

'Don't worry, Mum,' he said. 'It's only temporary, just for a week or two. She needs to think.'

What about? Flinch at the first pulled muscle and you'll never complete the marathon. Think too much and you don't *do* anything about a problem. And I raged some more, this time at a god I didn't believe in.

Weeks turned to months, then a year, and she left him for good. And I had no rage left, just sadness. My heart ached for him in his lonely state. Who'd make a cup of tea for him, or a meal when he couldn't find a bean of energy? Who was there left to love him apart from me, forced to care from a distance down a heartless phone?

I needed action. Dismissing his need to mend in solitude, I flew down to see him, careful not to over-sympathise or even hint at my own problems; careful not to outstay my welcome. I even moved into a pub down the road so my maternal presence, calm and well-practised in diplomacy though it tried to be, wouldn't make him feel worse. But it did. And I understood some of the reasons his girlfriend had left. I saw what bloody hard work he was, rocking between troughs of depression and desperate remedies that would never work. When I caught him in a low, his stiffening at my presence carved chunks out of me. When I dared to try and ease him away from his next miracle cure, his complete shutdown sluiced even deeper. Oh yes, I rationalised that it was the affliction rather than him that had changed his character from sunny to black, but it still hurt. I came home to weep in private.

But over the next few months his health improved. Slowly, by millimetres rather than inches, I heard traces of my real son emerging, tiny whispers of hope based on minuscule but concrete steps. He'd endured ME for more than three years and at last felt he'd got it sussed.

Then, just when I dared to breathe again, came the threat to the only thing he had left – his home. His ex-girlfriend was very sorry, and I do believe she was, but she needed her share of the assets tied up in their house. She wanted her own, even though it meant them selling up and making him homeless. Living totally on benefits by this time, he couldn't afford to extend the mortgage or fund a new one.

My imagination roared into life. He'd end up in a poky rented room, a dark, gloomy and probably damp hole where he'd never mend. He'd be surrounded by poor unfortunate no-hopers and sink into a bog of depression so low he'd be hospitalised.

Like most mother hens, I flapped into battle. 'Never, never, never will I allow you to be homeless,' I told him. 'I will not have you on the streets. I will sell my soul to keep you in your home.'

And I think I heard him smile. 'Thanks, Mum, but I'm okay, and I'd hate it if you restricted your life to fund mine. I do have pride, you know.'

I think I said 'Bollocks', or some such juicy word, and he laughed. A wondrous sound. Not the guffaw of old but definitely a whisper of one.

I didn't sell my soul of course, or my body, just handed over half my income and what little capital I had. Who needs money when it gives someone you love not a house but a home, somewhere to hide and mend and feel secure? Something to tend and fiddle with and paint when scraps of inclination and energy happen along. And he found them that year. He'd phone to tell me he'd cut his tiny patch of lawn or pruned a long-neglected shrub. He phoned to say he'd plastered that hole over his front door – you know the one I mean, Mum, the one that lets the rain in when it comes from the south. And then he phoned to tell me he'd not achieved much more in the DIY department, but that he'd enrolled on an FE course. 'I can't work full time yet, but I want to get out and do something. It's just a morning or two, and will be a good test of my stamina. I want to learn, Mum. I want to be out there. I want— ' His list of wants stretched into the far distance but, for the first time in years, he was pointing in the right direction.

I sang, in private. I dared to hope. It would still be a long time before he could start to take up where he'd left off, but at least he had a future and could see its glint.

The whole episode left me exhausted. Of course I battled on in stoic cheerfulness, decimating my own shrubs and hiding behind the roar of the mower. I managed my friend's moods and despair and relished her moments of hope, but overall I found contentment in chivvying us along our usual bumbling path. And sometimes when I watched the birds, I was up there swooping with them instead of merely admiring them.

A Hard Lesson

Rosie Pearce

We should have read the signs. Our eldest son (one of five), aged fifteen, was giving an excellent impression of the character Gaelan in the television series *The Planet of the Apes*. He simply gave up speaking in the house – well, certainly to us, his parents. He just grunted! I am not able to say what was happening in school or in the company of his friends and siblings. Since there were no adverse comments from his teachers, I can only suppose he was behaving normally outside the house.

Today it would no doubt be possible to surf the internet to compare problems and seek advice, but during the seventies there seemed to be no information or previous experience to guide us.

One thing he made obvious was that he hated sharing everything with his brothers and sister. He conveyed the message that he felt all the family treats and goodies – such as they were – should be his of right.

'I was the first child. Why did you have to have more?' he would ask occasionally. 'I want to be the only child.'

I tried to explain that as an only child myself, I could say with utter conviction it was a very lonely life, and that he did not know how lucky he was to have a large wrap-around family. My predictions that his brothers and sister would turn out to be his best friends and most reliable supporters in future fell on deaf ears.

When my son was about fourteen, we all went on a family camping holiday to Cornwall. On the cliffs at Land's End, he and I sat closely together, away from the others. For a few all-too-brief minutes we shared the magical experience of the rugged solitude and peace. Then, as suddenly, the moment was gone.

Even now, after almost thirty years, I treasure that memory.

On our return home, everything reverted to its old familiar pattern, and I was at the end of my tether. After more heart-wrenching private discussion, my husband and I decided the time had come to stop battling alone and seek professional advice. The domestic situation was having an adverse effect on the other children, with the eldest subversively commanding one hundred per cent of our time and attention. We made an appointment with Social Services.

At this point, I should explain the make up of our family. I lost my first husband in a farming accident in February 1971. At that time my children were aged six, four and almost two. It was a very traumatic period, but I did not believe the children were old enough to understand or be affected by the upheaval in their lives. I struggled to keep their daily routine going as normally as possible, sending the eldest to the village school as usual each day. We had to move out of our tied agricultural cottage, and later moved house a second time.

To cut a very long story short, I met my second husband, who had two small children, and we decided to bring up the five between us. With hindsight I often ask myself if all the changes in our lives within such a short period were to play their part in the sad situation in which we later found ourselves.

To return to the story, we were at a loss to find a solution ourselves. Perhaps we were too close to the day-to-day happenings. The fact was, our eldest son's sulky silences, which could last a week or more, were beginning to take their toll on the well-being and education of the other children.

The Social Worker did his best, and even suggested I needed to lighten up a bit and not take life so seriously. He drew up contracts of behaviour between ourselves and our son. We struggled to uphold our side of the bargain, but there was very little effort or interest from our son.

In the end he broke several days' silence to suggest his own answer. In front of the Social Worker he suddenly announced, 'I want to be adopted by another family.'

We argued, we reasoned, we pleaded, all without success. To our dismay the Social Worker was in favour of the idea. I was bitterly disappointed and felt deeply ashamed of my obvious failure as a mother. I battled against this solution, but had to agree in the end, as there was no workable alternative.

Years later, we learned that during this period our son was hiding spare clothes in a hedge down the lane. At nights when we thought he was in his room, he would climb out of the window, change his clothes and head off into town to meet other lads, to smoke, hang around bus shelters and playing fields, and eye up the local girls.

One fateful day, the Social Worker announced he had found a suitable family willing to foster our son. I was distraught at the news. I simply could not believe we had disintegrated so badly as a family. I can remember driving the ten miles to work each morning with so many tears filling my eyes I could scarcely see the road. It was very dangerous, but it was the only part of the day I could be completely alone and could stop putting on a brave face. It was very difficult to concentrate on my work in a laboratory without breaking down into tears. I suffered terrible embarrassment at being proven such a poor mother. I was unable to discuss my problems with anyone else, and did not want anyone to find out things had gone so badly wrong at home.

After my son left our home, we were encouraged to keep in contact, but to tell the truth, the situation was unnatural and awkward on both sides. But we persevered. At home, the other children's lives returned to some sort of normality, as in so many ways they had been deprived of our attention, since everything had focused on the one boy.

Over the following months and years, from this heart-breaking situation came more respect for the opinions and feelings on each side. We seemed to find the time and space to make an effort to understand each other's motives. In time, my eldest son had children of his own and then married (in that order!). He also bought his own house and we were more than willing to offer help where needed. Now, after almost twenty-five years, the bridges have been rebuilt and relations are as good as they are in any average family.

Just recently came a codicil to this story. My daughter said to me, 'Do you know my brother is grateful to you for being able to do the right thing for him? He said that without the experiences he had he would not be the person he is today. He told me because you were able to let him go, he learned to stand on his own two feet and got where he is now, buying his own house and being independent.'

I learned a hard lesson, too. I learned that parents and children have to grow apart before they can grown together again. But sadly, even now, I have never been able to discuss that period of our lives with my son. Why? I do not know. Perhaps I am just too afraid of opening up old wounds.

The Rocky Road to Motherhood

Amber Fleetwood

As a child, I had a dislike of dolls. Presented by well-meaning relatives at birthdays and Christmas, they invariably failed to engage my interest. By the time I was old enough to sew and to make things for myself, my favourite game was to create characters from stories out of scraps of felt, arrange them on my bedroom floor and escape with them into a world of adventure that absorbed me for hours.

Having babies seemed worlds away, something other girls aspired to, but not me. When I reached my teens, my parents impressed upon me the need to ignore boys until I was older, and concentrate on passing my exams in order to secure a good career. They seemed anxious to steer me away from the inevitability of becoming a wife and mother, and while their advice undoubtedly stemmed from a desire to avert a teenage pregnancy in the family, it fixed in my mind the notion that motherhood was something intended for other women, not me.

In my early twenties and recently married, I began to experience furtive baby cravings. I would stare wistfully and guiltily at shop window displays of Babygros, prams and other accoutrements of motherhood. They appeared to me to be forbidden fruit, holding an almost mystical significance, like sacred objects of a religion I could take no part in. This feeling was exacerbated when, my husband and I having decided to try for a baby, I experienced my first miscarriage a mere two months into the pregnancy.

Shaken but determined, we waited the required amount of time for my body to heal before trying again. This time I was three months into the pregnancy before miscarrying. I was devastated by this second failure to do what my body was surely made to do, and my husband and I agreed to stop trying for a baby, convinced that we were unable to become parents. I was ignorant then of other women's experiences of miscarriage, or how common it can be, even among women who have given birth to healthy children. I felt totally alone in my misery, even though my husband pointed out that he had also lost the babies.

My desire for a child became submerged – one of those things one never talks about because they are too painful. Several years later, my husband and I separated and my longing for a child resurfaced with a vengeance. Feeling alone in the world, and desperate for a home and family, I wondered if I had missed my chance. I was now at the age when people were beginning to wonder why I had no offspring and whether I had chosen to be childless. They would sometimes ask me thoughtless questions about it, which I found painful and difficult to answer. I affected a nonchalant air to conceal my anguish.

When I formed a new relationship, we decided to try for a baby straight away. I conceived very quickly, and was both excited and terrified. I was determined to ensure that everything worked out this time. The first four months passed and I began to relax a little. There was now a good chance that I would actually bear this child. I minimised the amount of stress I had to deal with, so as to keep the growing baby safe from possible triggers of miscarriage. It was not until I was six months pregnant and felt confident of carrying the baby to term that I presented myself to a doctor. He was annoyed with me for waiting so long before seeking medical attention, but I felt I had done the right thing, as I found the ante-natal sessions caused me much anxiety. First I was told I wasn't gaining enough weight, then later that I was gaining too much. The doctor talked to me as though my IQ was diminishing in direct proportion to my increase in girth. I was tired all the time, suffered a lot of back pain and felt emotionally volatile.

All these woes were in stark contrast to the information I was reading on motherhood. The books had inspiring titles such as *Naturebirth* and *Spiritual Midwifery* and contained beautiful photos of beaming mothers-to-be proudly cradling their rotund bellies and looking the picture of health. I felt heavy, stressed and uncomfortable. Where was I going wrong?

Fearing that the prospect of a "mechanised" birth was increasing my stress levels, I investigated the possibility of delivering at home. My local Birth Centre helpfully told me how to go about this. It was there that I learned for the first time of other women's experiences of miscarriage, which I found quite cathartic.

When I conveyed my intention to my doctor, he was horrified. He cited my age – thirty – and the fact that I was, in the parlance, an "elderly primagravida". He declared that I was putting my baby at risk, which upset me very much. That was the last thing I was trying to do.

Discouraged, I returned to the Birth Centre for consolation and advice. They told me my experience was not unique, and to persevere, which I did. My doctor was probably alarmed at the prospect of presiding over a home delivery, as he hadn't done one since his student days, and also it was fairly difficult to find a midwife prepared to attend one.

I stood firm, but with the necessary equipment already in my bedroom and the baby several days overdue, my blood pressure rocketed. My doctor insisted I go to hospital "for observation".

All my dreams collapsed. I realised that if I didn't begin labour soon, I would be induced and very likely experience the opposite of the kind of birth I had hoped for.

One of the Birth Centre women, an acupuncture trainee, visited me in hospital that evening. She offered to use acupuncture to induce labour. It would be gentler and less restrictive of my movement than a hospital induction, so I agreed. Having obtained permission from the hospital staff, my friend began the treatment there and then – inserting needles into my toes! The treatment concluded, my friend departed, promising to visit the next day.

I settled down to rest, but shortly began to experience mild labour pains. They soon became more insistent, so, having informed my partner and the midwife, I removed to the dayroom, so as not to disturb the women sleeping in the ward. My partner arrived quickly and helped by rubbing my back between contractions, which were now quite painful. I was pacing the dayroom floor in order to speed up labour, but it became increasingly difficult to stand on my tired and trembling legs. The excruciating pain of many hours of labour began to take its toll, and when at last my waters broke and the midwife said it was time to go to the delivery room, I was glad to lie down.

I was by now totally exhausted and my contractions slowed right down. An oxytocin drip was administered and the contractions resumed with frightening intensity. The pain was unbearable and I was glad to have gas and air. The baby began to move downwards at last, then stuck! The situation had become critical, as I was far too exhausted to push. For the sake of my now endangered baby, I agreed to a forceps delivery.

Through a haze of pain and weariness, I became aware of a red, dishevelled object being laid on my belly. My son! There are no words to describe how I felt as I looked at him for the first time. After a twenty-four-hour descent into hell, I had returned triumphant, cradling new life in my arms.

Speechless

Kim Davies

'You do realise assessment does not mean help, don't you?' Lucy patronised. Then she dropped her carefully worded bombshell 'Even if there's a problem it'll be months before you get help.' It did its job as she'd intended. I couldn't believe it. It didn't make sense.

Her words hung in the air before they struck. They twisted and turned until all that was left spinning round my head was 'No help. No help! No help!!'

That was all it took to silence me. There was nothing left to say. All my arguments were useless. Why prove there was a problem if there was no help?

The defences I had slowly built up fractured. I wanted to shout. To scream. But I pressed my lips tight – swallowed the words I wanted to hurl back at her. I closed the door and wandered through to the living room and sat down. I got up again. Stood looking about me. Felt the trap closing in. I began to prowl. Stalked from one room to another.

All the anguish of the past two years flowed through my body. I wanted to fight for my son, but how? The system was too big, too strong for me. There was no hope.

I was his mother. I knew there was more to it than Mart just being a little slow. Why wouldn't anyone listen? Why didn't anyone care? Every little hurt of the past two years pounded through me.

On that first visit from Helen, the health visitor, Mart was eighteen months and he wasn't talking. She sat there and told me not to worry. Oh no he wasn't slow, nothing unusual there.

And she sipped her tea, smiled and changed the subject. And I believed her. After all, she was the professional.

I could see her at all the other visits marking off the Denver chart. Mart performed well – he built his towers, caught a ball, pointed out colours, selected numbers, placed toys under, over and behind as instructed – until he got to speech.

She tried to be friendly and reassuring, repeated her "don't worry" messages and gave me little talkings-to. Told me second children were often later talking. Told me they were often lazy. Told me not to compare him with others.

Two came and went. Two and a half came and went. Three came and went and there was still no sign of any words, and no sign of any support, or any belief in what I was saying. But at each visit her smile became rather more fixed.

I wanted to shout that she was wrong, but I kept quiet. I couldn't explain. I couldn't refute her arguments. I didn't know why I was convinced there was a problem but I knew. There was something different about Mart, something not right.

The last time I saw her she sat resting her hands on her swelling belly. She couldn't leave without one last lecture and she excelled herself. 'Although I've never met one, some children don't talk till they're five'. I couldn't believe it. Of course she hadn't – it's not exactly usual.

But there was no point in causing a scene. I was hoping the new person would be more helpful. I'd borne welcome in my eyes every time I'd seen her, hoping for a sign of support and help. As she left I wished her well with a smile on my face while the serpent in my heart wished her all the anguish she'd put us through.

Not that my time had been wasted. I'd been busy finding out about language acquisition. I'd read books, spoken to experts, and written to them. They were all sympathetic, some empathetic even. But they'd all spoken of shortages of speech therapists. Some gave me encouragement. 'Keep at it. Press for a place on the waiting list. Keep a record of any noises and attempts at speech he makes.' And that's what I'd done.

My fists clenched as I remembered the last time Mart went to playgroup. When I went to fetch him, he was sitting at a table with the playleader. She was pointing to pictures in a book, trying to get him to name the objects. At the sight of me, Mart had rushed out while she tried to make out it was a bit of fun. 'We've been learning to talk, haven't we Mart?', but he was hiding behind me, his eyes cast down and lips clamped tight. After that he refused to go.

I almost relaxed as I remembered the hope when I found out that I could make a parent's referral. Not that any of the professionals had told me. A friend, Jim, worked for the Health Authority and had made some discreet enquiries. I could hardly answer him. I could have hugged him for the hope he'd given me. I sat down, wrote straight away, and posted it the next day.

I waited. And waited. And waited. But I heard nothing. There was no magic place on a waiting list. Not only was no-one listening, no-one was reading my letter. That's when I went to the local MP.

I soon got a response from that. A phone call from the Head of Speech Therapy. Once more I was told of the shortage of therapists and of the waiting list.

'But I've been waiting. I sent in a parent's referral.' There was a pause.

'We've never received a letter from you.'

The silence was from me that time. Then I found my voice. 'What do you mean never received it? I posted it weeks ago.'

'We never got it.'

'I wrote because the health visitor kept saying there was no need to worry. Well I am worried. It's nearly two years we've been trying to convince her we needed a referral.'

She finally agreed to put us on the list. I should have shouted and screamed to be put at the top of the list but I was so pleased I kept quiet. At last we were on the waiting list. We were going to be seen. We'd get help for his problem and life would become normal again.

It wasn't too long afterwards that Lucy, Helen's replacement, turned up. Mart had turned three and a half. I greeted her warmly and when she'd finished marking off the Denver chart we started to talk about the speech problem. I was able to speak the jargon by then. I was armed with theories and facts and stages of development and pressed her to agree that there was a problem. My knowledge threatened her position as the professional and she began to close up, but I never noticed. When she'd calmly dropped her bombshell it had been so effective.

I was still churning over all the pain and frustration of the last couple of years when the phone went. It was Andy. 'How did it go then? Any news of an appointment?'

That was the cue for the words to flow. I couldn't stop. I repeated all the worries and fears we both lived with every day. Nothing he hadn't heard before. I could hear the helplessness in his voice, 'I can't do anything from work. Why don't you phone the department and check out what she said?'

So I did. I phoned the Head of Speech Therapy, the one who'd finally put us on the waiting list. I sat on the bottom of the stairs, rehearsed what I would say, and breathed deeply, willing myself to relax.

'I just wanted to check when we'd be getting our appointment for Mart.'

Her voice was distant, impatient almost, 'As I've explained before…'

I fought to steady my voice. 'But I've just been told that we'll still be waiting after assessment. That there won't be any help even then.'

'It's not as straightforward …'

'But he'll be starting school in a year.' The waves of panic began to overcome the façade of control. I tried to rein back the mounting hysteria but the images of Mart alone in the classroom, not able to speak, were floating before my eyes. Images of him in a special school. Images of him without any friends. Who wants a friend who can't speak?

My voice faltered 'What'll happen then?' The tears began to roll down my face. 'How will he cope?' I managed to stutter before the waves of despair swept over me. Still sitting on the stairs, I curled into a foetal position, laid my head against the wall and cried. Deep tears, torn from the depth of my being. Inconsolable. Unable to speak.

How long did I sit there? A few seconds, a minute, two minutes? I don't know. I slowly became aware of snatches of a faint far away voice. It was coming from the receiver still clutched in my hand. The voice kept repeating 'Are you still there? Don't hang up. Are you still there? Don't hang up.'

And with each repetition I was slowly pulled back, the voice at the other end becoming stronger and more distinct. 'Don't hang up. We'll sort something. Are you listening?' Eventually I found a feeble response

'Yes.'

'We'll arrange an assessment.'

'When'

'Soon. The therapist for your area is in a meeting. She'll call you – today.'

Before the end of the afternoon it had all been arranged. Liz would come to the house the following Wednesday and undertake the assessment. I was drained. I could hardly take in how quickly everything had happened. Too tired to celebrate.

But the speed of reaction was not lost on me. Tears. That was what it had taken in the end. Tears. What if I'd been the type to throw a tantrum? What if I'd cried weeks, months, a year ago? Would we already have been well on the road to success? Was it all my fault? I should have shouted and screamed a long time ago. Should not have listened to their professional opinions. Should have believed my own instincts. No-one knew my son as I did. Why had I believed them?

*

I watched Liz approach the house. She looked wary as if wondering what awaited her, wondering how this mad mother would behave. She knocked on the door and turned away waiting for me to answer. By the time I opened the door she was the professional. Any sign of nervousness had gone.

I put on a video for Mart while Liz and I sat by the dining room table, warmed by the bright June sun streaming in through the window. She asked me questions about Mart's speech and I produced the records I'd kept.

She was impressed and listened carefully to everything I told her. From the usual babbling and early approximations of words, to the growing reticence to speak, the small list of sounds that acted as words but meant nothing to anyone else. "Wow" for brother, "ee ee" for the cat and "ee ee ah" when he wanted *The Three Little Pigs* read to him.

At last someone was listening, listening properly. She empathised with the daily struggle to communicate, the tantrums when I misunderstood, the times I couldn't understand at all and he wore himself out with his rage, the growing silences.

We went through to the living room. Mart was wary, reluctant to be drawn. But her alter ego appeared, a puppet, a mischievous monkey who joined in all the games she wanted him to play. Mart was beguiled and started performing all the tasks just as he had done for Helen and Lucy. He built towers, pointed at pictures, did jigsaws. But he did them one handed. His other hand hovered over his mouth, trying to hide it from Liz's scrutiny.

Afterwards we returned to the dining room. 'Don't mention it,' she said. 'Don't ask him to speak. Tell him it doesn't matter.'

I gasped. I wasn't in the habit of lying to anyone, let alone my children.

'You have to. He knows there's something wrong. He's beginning to show signs of withdrawal.'

'But of course it matters. How can we cope? Life's difficult with the misunderstandings. The tantrums.'

'You need to speak without words. You must learn to use

gestures. That'll help build up his confidence as well as easing the daily struggle.'

'What about the future? How will he learn to speak if we sign?'

'Say the words as you sign. Don't stop talking to him. But don't pressure him to talk to you.'

'Supposing he doesn't follow our example and start speaking?'

'Children want to talk. It's part of their nature. He's not being lazy or wilful – you know that. When the time's right for him he will speak.'

It was so difficult. I so wanted Mart to speak. To be like all the others. I started again 'But...'

'For now reassure him and give him the alternative to speak with his hands. That will help tremendously.'

I'd waited a long time for this help. I had to believe her. I swallowed back my objections.

'How do we learn?'

'You know my time's limited? If I send you information and the diagrams, will you practise them with him? Then I can come and see his progress in a month.'

I nodded. Promised to do it regularly, every day. If that was what was needed, that's what we would do. 'But what about the long term?'

'He has a form of oral dyspraxia. He can make most of the sounds he needs – he just can't sequence them into words. The sounds he struggles with we can work on – later. For now he just needs to play. We'll play games to encourage more mouth movement – blowing bubbles, blow football that sort of thing. Play Simple Simon – it'll help his sequencing skills – let him win and praise him.'

Her diagnosis made and the beginning of a strategy in place, Liz stood to leave. 'There's definitely a problem. A problem that's beginning to have a knock on effect. I wish I'd seen him a couple of years ago.'

There was silence. I gasped. A scream reverberated around my head but all I could force out of my lips was a very soft 'And me.'

The Unsevered Cord

Brenda Curtis

The baby sucked in its first breath giving a lusty yell that turned its body from purple to bright pink. I wiped its eyes and mouth, clamped, tied, and cut the gristly, translucent, cord and wrapped the baby in a towel. I handed the bundle to the mother and she gathered her new baby into the crook of her arm and gazed, exhausted, into its blinking eyes. The baby was freed from the womb, but the mother will never be free again. As a midwife, motherhood was my business and I developed a particular sympathy for mothers. I had realised that most babies have an insatiable greed for survival but suspected, from observation of my own mother's life, that the mothers would have the greater struggle.

Then it was my turn. Life picked me up, whirled me round, and by the time I was thirty, found myself with husband, home, three children under four and a part-time career, working night shifts at weekends. For five tumultuous years, if my womb wasn't nourishing a foetus, my breasts secreted milk and my vagina invariably accommodated a penis. The boundaries of my body had been breached. There was the shock of conception, the feeling of being trapped, the knowledge that a bundle of cells was rapidly multiplying within my body and that there was no escaping the ordeal of pushing a fully formed baby through the narrow channels of my own pelvis. Every woman knows that at the moment of birth, there is always the possibility of death.

Motherhood for me was primarily physical. I was work embodied. It started with the hard labour and ecstatic orgasm of childbirth and continued through the pain of engorged breasts and sore nipples to the rapture of lying on my bed in the silence of an afternoon with my firstborn latched onto a breast, enjoying the sensation of his regular pull and swallow. He lets go, the moist nipple bounces away, he looks up at me and his milk-blistered lips part in a wide smile. There was the endless task of stirring dirty nappies in a steaming copper boiler to the bliss of bathing and soaping his silky soft skin and of holding him against my shoulder, powdered, replete, smelling his vanilla warmth and feeling his little puffs of breath against my neck. The first time I wheeled my baby out, I felt luminous. Why weren't people turning to stare? I felt unique.

We moved to a flat in a house on a steep hillside where I had to haul the pram up six steep steps. One winter's day, I had just reached the front door when I let go of the handle. Standing on the top step, I watched the pram tip and tumble and land upside down on the path at the bottom. There was silence. This had not happened...turn the clock back... I rushed down the steps to extricate my baby, terrified of what I might find. I found him awake, blinking, his small face peering out at me from a cocoon of blankets, surprised to be so suddenly roused from sleep. The raised hood and fixed apron of the pram had prevented him from being flung onto the hard concrete. Clutching him to my thumping chest, I went indoors trembling. This might have been my first ghost child, floating forever in limbo, at the end of a very short cord. Twenty-three years later, he stretched that cord again when, in dismay, I watched him disappear down the stairs into the dark cavern of an underground station with a backpack that towered above his head. He was going travelling and had no idea of a destination except the compulsion to follow his karma. Twenty-three more years and he continues his quest but Chopin and Bach have been exchanged for goats and horses and his pianists fingers are calloused from rough work.

The attachment to my own mother was no less strong. However much I wished to break away from her influence, her subliminal messages were well learned. As a young, single woman, she'd had a good job, had bought her own home, a rare thing for a woman in the early 1930s, until, at the age of thirty, her life changed when she fell for a tall, attractive, amusing soldier, ten years older than herself. They married but there were no photos of their wedding and, as a child, I learned that there were questions not to be asked. I pieced together her silent history only after she had died when I saw, from the date on her marriage certificate, that she was three months pregnant. I grew up aware of a legacy of bitterness and when I was told that she had died, a wild, primitive wail erupted from a deep place within me. I sat quietly by her body, thinking how smooth and peaceful her face was, with the frowns and worry lines of anxiety erased. For a brief moment, I felt a sense of release, as though I was wearing no seat belt, but, very soon, I felt the tug of the cord. The link was intact and she floated, still floats, freely, in and out of my head. I continue to hear the impatient pitch of her voice, taste her hot jam roly-poly puddings and feel her presence in unexpected moments.

I was daughter, then mother, and my mother became grandmother. She came to help me when I had my three babies, as I later went to help my daughter when she had hers. Soon after my second child was born, I remember kneeling, marooned in the bath, breasts like red hot footballs, jets of milk spurting into the bath water, listening to the thump of my electric iron as Mum ironed sheets downstairs. She was used to a flat iron that had to be heated on a gas flame and brought down heavily to remove creases. I was grateful for her help but resentful that she was running my home and irritated by her familiar habits and mannerisms. When it was my turn to help my daughter, I could see that, in the same way, my presence on her territory annoyed her, she wanted me to go, and she wanted me to stay. The cord stretched but did not break and has narrowly survived many such ebbs and flows of love and rejection. This second child had grown up feisty and rebellious. On one occasion, she turned her face to the wall, spurning love, but on another, when my handbag was stolen on a shopping trip, she gave me my return fare home, and, going to her makeup purse, took out her lipstick, saying, 'Here Mum, take this.' Now a grown woman, I look in wonder at her fullness, her sexiness, geranium lips, face glowing beneath white angora beret with sparkly brooch, and the grace with which she steps out in her long burgundy leather coat, and I admit to a pang of jealousy. My daughter gnaws at the cord that binds but I, too, sometimes wish to be free of this burden of love.

I had my babies in the early 1960s. New sexual freedoms were emerging but the freedoms offered by contraception had not kept pace. I remember the painful frustration between fulfilment of spontaneous desire and the desperate fear of becoming pregnant again. A fourth baby in six years would hardly have been welcome. If this was difficult for me, how much harder it must have been for my mother. My third child was born in the bedroom of my childhood. We were between houses and my parents agreed I could arrange for the confinement to take place in their home. It was only years later that I began to appreciate any misgivings they might have had because they were both still working, even though my father was then seventy years old. The cords that bound us all held fast, and I moved into their small, terraced house, very pregnant, trailing two toddlers, while my husband worked and house hunted over one hundred miles away.

We moved to rural Gloucestershire and I lived in a state of perpetual motion. There was no privacy in the lavatory, in the bath, or in bed. I stirred saucepans with a baby tucked under one arm or an infant's legs clamped round my waist. I sucked bruised fingers, kissed bumped heads, stuffed stiff little arms into winter coats, read stories, headed off tantrums and played diversionary games. I cooked food that disappeared too quickly, cleaned things that preferred to be dirty, and spent long stretches of tedium in parks and playgrounds. Images of the faces of laughing children are burned onto my retina and my ears still ring with their cries of delight or rage. Those years are now memories, but I vividly remember what seemed to be the unendingness of motherhood. The most difficult task of all was negotiating between the conflicting demands of five individuals, the nurturing and getting to know the personalities of each child, learning the idiosyncrasies of my husband, managing a part-time job and trying to maintain a social life for myself. It is called "having it all". Something had to give and, for a short while, it was my mental health. My daughter remembers the chink of ice in my whisky glass. It was the thought of the children that brought me back from the brink. Years later, my youngest child was to say that he wished he hadn't had such a happy childhood and I think he glimpsed what it had cost.

This third child was all laughter and energy. Anchored in the pram, he would bounce it on its springs to where the action was. Now grown, he walks into a room, all lean six feet of him, and the sun comes out. Endowed with a generous spirit, he has developed deep insight into his own and other people's psychology. His is the eye behind the camera. When he was nineteen, about to embark on an important year at college, it was again necessary that we move job and home. We installed him in a student bed-sit with purple flocked wallpaper and removed ourselves to London. The wallpaper was the last straw and he soon moved himself elsewhere. He still likes to amuse people with a tall story about how his parents abandoned him. I think it hurt but he is a survivor.

I am amazed at the alchemy that transformed the girl I was, to the woman I now am, and how my babies, whose small bodies and moods I knew so intimately, are adults about whom I know so little. I could soothe my infant's hurts but there isn't much I can do about their mid-life crises, except be at the end of the cord when they need me.

The Birth of Misha

Jane Burnham

9th November 1980

(*At the time of Misha's birth I was living with my partner, Andrew, and my daughter, Emily, in a remote Sussex cottage. We were trying to lead as self-sufficient a lifestyle as possible and had no car, no telephone, and no central heating*)

Early to bed as we had had a late night the previous one and I had been out all day doing my Christmas shopping. All this walking and a deep desire to make love must have started it all off as I woke at 3.00am, at first thinking nothing of it, being used to waking several times in the night during the last couple of months of my pregnancy. I gradually became aware of stomach cramps, an exceedingly damp warm nightdress, a need to get up and empty my bowels...although it was eleven days early, there was no doubt in my mind that this was it. I got back into bed and lay for a while timing contractions (already two minutes apart) before waking Andrew.

We got up, gently pottered around, and drank a quiet cup of tea. Or rather, I think I just looked at mine, simply taking it all in. There was a sense of suppressed excitement as we sat very quietly. At 4.30am Andrew set off into the dark on his bicycle to the nearest phone box to phone the midwife. He must have savoured a pleasing sense of our rustic way of living as he went pedalling along the dark silent lane, peering into the dim torch beam. It was a beautifully still and quiet night.

But from that moment on everything seemed a mad flurry. Why wasn't I more organised beforehand? Old linen and plastic sheets on to the bed, log fire to be lit in the bedroom, dressing table to be cleared for the midwife's use, clothes to be put to air for the baby...all this, stopping every two minutes to cope with contractions which were now lasting longer and needing level-two breathing. I was also walking around with a towel between my legs as my waters were leaking fast. Andrew, back from the phone box, was giving me lots of support, calmly getting everything ready, and cuddling me during contractions. There was a feeling of great excitement and togetherness.

It was an hour later before the midwife arrived. Although we had never met her before, it was a great relief to see her, and we felt an immediate sense of friendliness and confidence from her. Her examination showed me to be six centimetres dilated, so Andrew was once again sent off into the dark to phone the doctor and his parents. Contractions were now coming really fast and were very painful, but I was coping all right with level-three breathing. At this point I had to lie down on the bed.

At 6.30am a sleepy, bewildered Emily woke up and was carried in to say hello to me, just as Andrew's parents arrived to look after her, shortly followed by the arrival of Dr King, carrying a pair of forceps. Andrew got them on the boil on the kitchen range (one *does* need boiling water for a home delivery!). My contractions were by this time very strong, but I was still coping. My memories were of Andrew dashing in and out, making cups of tea for everyone, stoking up the fire. How comforting and homely it was to watch the flicker of the flames. He fetched and carried endless towels, all the time giving me words of encouragement.

About 7.00am I felt an urge to push. The midwife examined me again and said there was still an anterior lip and I mustn't push. I was beginning to lose control, shaking all over, feeling sick, but Andrew was by my side, holding me, breathing with me, making me breathe, and it needed all my strength to fight off that tremendous urge to push. The midwife examined me again and I remember clearly her words: "Good news for you, Jane, you can push now.' That was 7.30.

What a relief! Everyone helped prop me up on numerous cushions and pillows, and I felt great excitement as I pushed with the next contraction. After what I'd been told about second babies I was expecting this one to slither out with the first push! But it was not to be so. After half an hour, although I was so nearly there, I felt I was making no more progress, and Dr King suggested forceps. I didn't feel any fear or trepidation at the mention of forceps. Everything seemed to have happened so fast and furious that I had not had time to get on top of it, and I now just wanted it to be over. Perhaps stronger was the feeling of having let Andrew down by not being able to manage alone, though this feeling did not last long.

I was moved down to the end of the bed. Dr King was kneeling on the floor, a midwife on either side (Miss Castle, the chief midwife had just arrived on the scene). Andrew was kneeling on the bed beside me, which left not an inch to move in our tiny bedroom. How far removed from the sterile hospital environment!

I didn't really feel the episiotomy, but having the forceps inserted was extremely painful. Dr King said afterwards he had only given me a half dose of local anaesthetic, but I didn't think to ask why. One more push was all that was needed and there he was, our beautiful baby, alive and well. He immediately let out the most delicious wonderful cry, a bursting proclamation of life and wellbeing. What a tremendous feeling flooded my soul.

'It's a boy!' I heard one of the midwives announce, and he promptly proved it by peeing all over Dr King! The cord was cut, the mucus sucked out and then what BLISS; in a matter of seconds he was lying peacefully on my tummy, nuzzling up to my breast but not yet interested in suckling, blinking his eyes at these new surroundings. All we could do was look at him and stroke him. Words cannot describe the beauty of that moment – the miracle of birth had left us elated, exhilarated and full of wonder.

Everything else seemed of little significance – the delivery of the placenta, the stitching up (during which the baby was taken into the kitchen to be bathed and dressed and introduced to his big sister and grandparents). There are then memories of lots of people in the bedroom, drinking cups of tea, Dr King with drenched, bloodstained trousers, and Emily climbing all over me and the baby.

The rest of the day was spent in a state of total euphoria, just indulging in the whole wonderfulness of birth. Emily went off with Andrew's parents, so Andrew and I were left alone with our newborn child. He was wide awake all day and so was I. Andrew was the most exhausted. That was such an important time for the three of us – a bonding together and setting up of a new relationship – a time we wouldn't have missed for anything. How different from the isolation I felt in hospital after Emily's birth. I definitely wouldn't have chosen anything other than a home birth.

Misha became a father for the first time in January 2007.

The Politician's Wife

Glenys Kinnock

I was living in Blackwood when my children were born at St
James's Hospital in Tredegar. Neil was elected when Stephen
was just six months old, so all our family life he was in politics.
What we didn't fully realise when he was first elected was that
Neil would be away all week, so all of a sudden I was on my own
with a baby.

I didn't cope well. Luckily, I had a lot of help from my parents-
in-law, who lived close by. They really were a rock to me. But in
the two weeks before Rachel was born in 1971 both Neil's parents
died. His father had a sudden heart attack and the following
week his mother died, quite literally, of a broken heart. No-one
realised she had heart problems and it was a terrible blow.

Neil was an only child, so we had two funerals to organise,
which meant Rachel's birth was very different to how things had
been for Stephen. It was at that point we decided we couldn't
live as we had been any more. We were a very close family
and the strain of separation was too much for both of us. In
1973 we decided to move to London, but keep a home in the
constituency.

Moving the family from the constituency is not something we
had intended to do when Neil was elected. But the local Labour
party accepted that this was the best thing for us as a family. So
for several years we commuted between London and our home
in Pontllanfraith, which was a terraced house that we went to at
weekends. The kids liked being there, but it became slightly more
difficult when they got older and wanted to do things with their
school friends at weekends in London.

Both the children went to the local comprehensive school in

London – we never sought any special treatment. We just wanted our children to turn out well and I think they have. Both of them are good, honourable, well-qualified people with happy families of their own.

But being married to an MP definitely wasn't easy. You have to accept big disruption. Neil always made a great effort, though, even when he became Leader of the Party, to be at parents' evenings, school concerts and sports games. The kids were proud of him being so loyal.

The press really seemed to hate me in those days. I've always been interested in politics and was involved in Greenham Common and the anti-apartheid movement, as well as Neil's election campaigns. The papers had me down as an aggressive feminist and dubbed me "Lady Macbeth". But my home life didn't reflect what was written in the press. I made sacrifices to be a mother. I resumed teaching while we lived in London – I taught for thirty years – but I suppose I could have achieved a lot more in that career if I'd been able to take all the opportunities.

I did a lot of supply teaching in order to be more flexible. The children were well into junior school by the time I got a full-time job. I became a specialist reading advisor in Brent schools, but I always felt I had to be there for my kids. Some people have criticised me for this. Natasha Walter, in her book, *The New Feminism*, complained that I was not practising the equality I preached. But we simply didn't have the money to afford the type of childcare that would have been needed. And anyway, I couldn't have coped with the guilt and anxiety I would have felt at being away from the kids if I'd taken on an onerous full-time job.

I was never not working, but it was only in the early '90s, when the kids were at University, that I thought about seeking election. While driving to South Wales Neil and I were talking about the fact that the sitting MEP for South East Wales was standing down, and I asked 'Who's going for the seat?' He mentioned a list of possibilities and I said 'I'll go for it'. He nearly drove off the road with surprise and delight. I just decided there and then. I think there comes a time when you feel you *can* do what you always wanted to do in your heart of hearts.

I've been in the European Parliament for twelve years now and I've been continually active, especially on constituency issues in Wales and on my speciality, international development and the fight against global poverty. When I was first elected I had the biggest individual majority ever – it was in the *Guinness Book of Records*! Everyone was so nice when it was announced. They said 'It's your turn now.' I've carved out my own career and I feel I have my own identity which I've earned through my own hard work.

Having said that, I'm almost as committed a grandmother as I was a mother. I love being around children. I often babysit for my children and have my house kitted out with cots and changing tables, books and toys. When I was first elected in 1994 Stephen's wife, Helle, was also elected as an MEP for Denmark. They had a home in Brussels so I saw both their babies the day they were born. It was lovely to be able to see so much of them, just as it is marvellous to have Rachel and Stuart's children near us now.

It is every woman's fate to be seen as someone's wife, mother, aunt, or grandmother. I've always been known as 'the wife of Labour MP Neil Kinnock', or 'the wife of the Leader of the Opposition', and later 'the wife of the former Labour Leader', but that's getting less and less now. In fact, Neil now says he calls himself 'the husband of Glenys Kinnock MEP'.

That said, I always remember that when I was first elected and my son was working as a research assistant at the Parliament, I was walking to my office in Brussels when I met another MEP who introduced me to the two young assistants who were with him as "Stephen's mum" – so some things never change!

It's All a Matter of Perspective

Gabriella Walsh

I found the whole unplanned nature of pregnancy a great surprise. I was used to a life where every moment was organised, planned, timetabled and in my control; suddenly I no longer knew my physical limits or when the great event would take place. I found I could walk down hill for miles but soon ran out of steam going uphill. I was amazed that when I climbed Cadair Idris at about six weeks pregnant I had to virtually crawl the last 500 yards to the top, gasping for breath. It was reminiscent of the time I had climbed Mount Kinabalu in Borneo where, at 4,000 metres, I was lacking in oxygen from the altitude-induced thin air. On Cadair my twin baked-bean size babies were stealing my oxygen!

I knew twins could quite commonly arrive any time onwards from 35 weeks as they run out of space... With my four foot waist and 4 stone weight gain I had to cross my fingers and hope they would stick it out until their 38 week booking for a Caesarean (on my niece's birthday, 1st August 1997).

The heat intensified and I could only waddle about desperate for cooler weather and fresh air. I felt a real sense of freedom when a week before they were born I took up a friend's offer of a spin out into the harbour in his double kayak – freedom of movement at last and a sneaking suspicion that dolphins have got their lifestyle issues sussed.

The joy of the twins arrival was masked by the extreme grogginess of post-general anaesthesia and the excruciating back pain and sciatica set off that morning by an untimely twisted lurch of my large body out of the rocking chair to answer an insistent phone call. The midwives were surprised by my back-pain-induced upright constipated-chicken walk as they were more used to the stooped Caesarean shuffle – in the pain stakes the back pain was in a league apart from the Caesarean.

It was a relief that my husband had witnessed the flood of my waters over the surgeon's white wellies and could testify to the babies' origins, as I can't say I instantly felt they were mine. I felt totally committed to looking after their every need but wasn't quite sure of the small print in the employment contract.

Fay settled down to breastfeeding well, however Zoe was slow to suckle and there started a rollercoaster of expressing milk, cup feeding, torturous tube feeding accompanied by angry screams, attempting to suckle, vomiting and weight loss. I felt devastated, inadequate and guilty as she lost a pound in weight and her wrist and leg ID bands dropped off her shrinking limbs. A round-the-clock three-hourly regime ensued of feeding Fay whilst expressing milk and then attempting to breast feed Zoe supplemented by a bottle of my milk. I somehow kept going through the mad cycle delighted as Zoe finally started to gain weight, my back pain settled and we were allowed home.

When they were 13 months old the back pain and sciatica returned with a vengeance, no doubt triggered by lifting increasingly heavy babies. At first I was still able to go to work, although I increasingly found myself giving lectures and tutorials whilst lying down. I finally had to give up. I spent about a year of my life lying on the floor. Unless you have a burning interest in tessellating ceiling tiles or carpet textures, it doesn't have a lot to recommend it as a position from which to conduct your daily life.

Meanwhile my husband took on shopping, cleaning, childminding, working and coping with a depressive chronic benign intractably pained wife. After a less than successful back operation I learned to accept a life where every morning I woke up to another day with a back that felt as though a truck had driven into it in the night and my leg burning as if it had been dipped in liquid nitrogen and was thawing out in the most unbearable manner. I spent most of my time stretched out on the sitting room rug playing floor games with the babies. Jigsaws were always a popular option. I loved to hear Fay's voice as she belly surfed down the stairs shouting "igso, igso, igso".

Rough and tumble had to be limited to micro-scale. A very fierce 'NO' borne of pain and fear as they came careering into me and they very soon learned not to. I feel terrible for the times I have roared in angry self-preservation when they have inadvertently bumped into me or caused me to flinch, sometimes resulting in a two week or more major flare up of the pain. I am so proud of them now for being so understanding and caring – often their response if I am cross and sharp tongued is to give me a cuddle and rub the "sore bit" of my back.

From that point on I never lifted them up and neither did my husband or the lovely Lyn who helped look after us. Thus they never learned that universal pre-speech 'I want to be carried' arms up gesture. I felt like a stranded whale eternally waiting for the miraculous tide to come in and give me freedom of movement again. For my children however, having a mother skewered to the living room floor, available for play at their level must have been heavenly. There was no need for them to cling to my ankles to distract me from purposeful domestic chores as I was always there for them and had by then learnt to live with dust and crumpled clothes. As lifting the babies into a pushchair and manoeuvring a pushchair were taboo (back unfriendly activities), establishing independent locomotion was an early priority.

I was so frustrated by my reliance on other people to be able to go anywhere as I could no longer drive comfortably. Each baby's attempt at self propulsion was eagerly applauded as I counted the moments until we could all be mobile again. I remember the excitement of our first independent adventure outside with Fay in little red wellies and Zoe in her cousin's old shoes tottering twenty yards down the lane to visit Billy the old he-goat in the barn down the road.

Gradually we built up our collective stamina until the babies overtook my capabilities. Reins were an essential part of the repertoire as I was unable to run after them. They tried lunging forward to swing on the reins, testing their boundaries with the undesirable side effect of jarring my back. I felt horribly uncaring but my instinctive defensive reaction was to let go with a resultant splat. It has to be said that they did learn to avoid pulling on the reins very quickly. There was a mixture of trepidation and excitement that surrounded those outings which is hard to explain. I was never quite sure if we could make it in one piece; it always felt as though we were pushing the boundaries of our capabilities.

I remember feeling very adventurous one day and setting off with a small rucksack, holding hands with a toddler on each side for the village shop, a mere 400 yards around the corner. We made it and I bought a pint of milk and headed for home. The previously unnoticed slight incline was now a notable obstacle to progress. Fay and Zoe started to head in opposite directions and I was literally at the end of my tether. Back pain searing, patience waning, I opted for Emergency Response Number One and lay on the pavement, explaining to the pair of them that we would wait to go home until they walked sensibly. Much to my amazement a car screeched to a halt and a man leapt out full of concern to ask if I was all right. When I explained I was fine but just resting my back he combined irritation and embarrassment into a frosty expression and muttered something about 'I s'pose you're not having a heart attack then', leapt back into his red Rover determined to put the sordid incident behind him. I meanwhile felt like a freak and was desperate to teleport back behind the privacy of my front door.

I steeled myself for a second attempt of the north face of the pavement and we made it up the hill without further incident. I was back on my carpet, exhausted but with a sense of achievement at having made it to the shop and back.

There were days when it felt as if I had landed a part in the panto from hell with a punishing schedule: performances required at all hours, (keeping the real me hidden) avoiding expressing my very real pain and the accompanying despair and sense of uselessness, focussing instead on the small achievable tasks of the moment – like changing a nappy or twelve a day.

My husband installed a step ladder in the utility room next to a large work top where I could change their nappies. Marooned on my carpet in the sitting room with my twin babies for most of the day I would, once the suspicion that a nappy change was due (confirmed by the sniff test), log roll onto my side and over onto my tummy, wince up onto all fours and climb up the furniture to reach standing position. I would then exhort them to crawl along the corridor to negotiate the step down to the expanse of ill-washed kitchen floor which received one polishing pass as they crawled through and on down the next step to the utility room and up the stepladder for a nappy change at a back-friendly waist height. They could climb up the step ladder onto the work surface before they could walk and more amazingly they did so under their own steam several times a day. They continued to climb up there for another year spending about an hour every morning learning to get dressed by themselves.

I am eternally grateful to Lyn who had the patience of a saint and would foster every move towards independence. It was like a military operation with a goal of minimising my required standing up time at all aspects of the day. Zoe took to the concept with great gusto "Do it self" she would screech and insist on putting her own tights on age fourteen months. If you tweaked one toe of the tights to line them up, she would have a screaming fit and rip them off and start again at which point I was also ready to have a screaming fit and speed the process up so I could lie down again.

Thankfully Lyn took them out to a playgroup for a couple of hours on some days. As the front door closed behind the three of them, I would breathe a sigh of relief and go through my relaxation exercises to help deal with the pain before making a plan for the rest of the day when I would be in sole charge. I would work out the best way to handle problem areas and dream up a few contingency plans. Routine was all important for me, pacing myself to make sure I didn't overdo it. I had great fun inventing games which involved me lying down whilst Fay and Zoe twirled around the room on special missions and strange variants of Simon Says.

From an early age Fay and Zoe were happy to snuggle one each side of me in bed while I read them a story. This was my fail-safe coping activity when standing up was no longer an option. I could lie down and relax, deriving great comfort from their cuddles as well as knowing where they were – safe and not up to mischief. On bad days I would read for hours. My greatest wish was for them to be able to sit on my lap as I read to them but it was too painful for me to sit for long on my own, let alone with additional weight, so lying down was the next best option.

Feeding time was an interesting affair, sitting shovelling teaspoons into the baby bird beaks would have been just possible for my ten-minute sitting tolerance level. However I soon discovered that Fay had a propensity to clamp her jaw shut which caused unacceptable delays in mealtimes so I resorted to the self-service option. Food supplies now designated "finger food" regardless of texture and consistency, merely on the basis of mode of consumption. I would dump the food in the moulded edged highchair tray and then lie down on my foam mat on the floor to recover after the trial of preparation – a new definition of fast food was anything that minimised standing up time. Pureed avocado and banana was a hot favourite with Zoe – particularly useful for hair sculpture. After an hour of eating/playing in their high chairs I was sufficiently rested to mop up after them before embarking on the next phase of the day.

Looking back I feel as though I had a strange experience of motherhood as I was constantly having to consider my pain management needs first and then mesh my children's needs in with them. My resurrection coincided with the development of my children. I felt subsumed into their world. They taught me to live in the here and now and to laugh at the ridiculous in the way only a toddler knows how. They provided quality distraction from the unrelenting business of living with chronic pain. I am delighted to have had an ankle's eye view of their world through that miraculous year from one to two years old when they learn to walk and talk and I learned to sit and walk again. I was advised very strongly by my consultant never to have any more children for my back's benefit so as I grieved for another decision about my future taken out of my hands, part of me savoured every moment, thankful for the two wonderful, happy, healthy daughters whose lives I had the privilege to share.

Birth at 47

Edith Thomas

'I'm pregnant,' I said and collapsed tearfully into my seventeen-year-old daughter's arms.

'Oh, Mum, how lovely!' With those words she banished the disaster of a sixth pregnancy at the age of forty-seven. From then on it was a joyful surprise, eagerly awaited. Hubby took the news calmly, when I explained how small this baby would be – as if he was unaware of the nature of babies. He had fathered five already.

My dreams were often troubled with putting my very tiny baby to sleep in a drawer and not being able to remember which one she was in. I would be frantically searching through the house. It was a very debilitating dream.

Our little daughter finally arrived by Caesarean, after the specialist decided that she would be normal. I had hoped for a natural birth, but was content with the decision because I knew the placenta was low. 'Don't touch me, or I'll break,' I thought, as they wheeled me from the theatre.

I wasn't allowed to eat for hours, so the ice cubes fed me by my eldest daughter cheered me and aided me in tentatively holding my new child. She was the smallest of all my babies, but not the tiny thing of my dreams, I was relieved to see. Holding her was a humbling experience. Another tiny life entrusted to my care – but this time would be different. I would have five young helpers – and Dad, of course.

She was so small and I was so old. I let her snuggle on the pillow between us, but I was so worried that I might smother her that I lay awake endlessly. Because of my medical history, she didn't have the whooping cough vaccination. She whooped,

I'm sure she did, and the nights were purgatory because on the hour she whooped, and I had to sit her up and have a basin ready. She didn't open her eyes, and mine were blurred, and remained so all night and day for weeks. The doctor would not diagnose it as whooping cough, but the nurses agreed with me. We found a homeopath doctor at Aberystwyth Hospital, and she finally responded to one of the treatments he gave her.

'Mum, what happened to Rhiannon's head?' asked her brother, returning from a few days away at camp. 'It's gone a funny shape.'

'Oh! You're right. She fell out of her high chair on Saturday.' I was devastated that I hadn't noticed my little treasure had hurt herself. Off to the doctor again, another referral to the hospital. But she didn't develop any distressing symptoms, so we went home the next day. I felt terribly guilty. I had never been a careless mother before. Was Rhiannon simply accident prone?

Starting school had never been a problem for my other children. I was thrilled that they were embarking on a new adventure. But Rhiannon's primary school was Welsh and her exposure to the language up to then had been minimal. I hated to leave her in a world she didn't understand, but I was comforted by the kindness of the staff, and one day she came home speaking Cymraeg!

When she was five, I started a part-time job, because my husband had become very stressed and I thought it was time I did some earning for the family. It pained me to leave my little one, yet I could not have left her with anyone I trusted more than her dad. Even though I wasn't there for her when she came home, three nights a week, I knew she was loved and cared for, and I was able to enjoy working in the world again.

At three she gave me a turn, when she did the splits for the first time. Later I loved watching her doing gymnastics – not so much a proud mum, as a delighted one, especially when she represented Dyfed in a national competition. It was the first time she had stayed away from home, even for one night, and we were both traumatised, even though she was nine years old by then. I made a nuisance of myself ringing up repeatedly to see if she was happy.

My admiration for her grew as she practised and practised to strengthen her body in order to do spectacular things with it. Gymnastic lessons cost more than we could afford, but when they came abruptly to an end because of an injury to her heel, I felt that life was empty – and I worried that she did too. But with secondary school came athletics and contemporary dance.

Again we were thrilled with her achievements and loved attending the various events. Our home was full of life – her life. She was always practising. 'Is that better, Mum, or shall I do it this way?' Always on the go. We encouraged, we comforted and we enjoyed the surprise that came to us in our later life.

At sixteen she left home to go to college. All was well. We collected her on Friday afternoons and brought her home, to have to ourselves. We caught up with what was happening at college, and then returned her on Sunday nights. Then she met a boy and didn't want to come home at weekends. He was a nice lad, but I was so jealous of him I did nothing but moan to my darling, until I'm sure she hated me. I had to give myself a talking-to, or I knew I'd lose her. It was hard to let her go; to let her live her own life without me to guide and nag her. I had to stand back and let her make her own mistakes.

Even now, when she is twenty-one, I hurt when she hurts. Nightly I toss in indecision, watching for the daylight, glad to rise, yet purposeless, because I cannot sort out her problems. She will rise above her difficulties, and I am sure that in the future she will delightfully surprise me again.

One Step at a Time

Daisy May

In the time it takes me to drive the two miles to the hospital, I am reacquainted with the pain of loss: a pain that grows in my stomach, that turns my breath shallow, that has me clinging to the steering wheel, and asking myself what I am doing here. I nudge the car between a laundry van and a rusty Ford Cortina, switch the engine off, slam the door shut, lock it, and go in search of the maternity unit. Two wrong turns later, down a poorly lit alleyway, up a few steps, and an automatic door swishes open to let me in.

I am not sure I want to do this. I dig my closed fists deeper into my trouser pockets, stare at my feet, and walk in.

I'll never make it to the end of the corridor. Tiny waves undulate over my thighs, and my legs are shaking. Bitter saliva fills my mouth. I heave. I'm going to be sick. A door opens to my right, and I can't help looking in. The bed is high on metal legs. A grotesque shape billows under pale green sheeting. A scream tears through the heat.

'Go on love, I can see the head.' The voice is male, solid, in control. A woman whimpers, groans, sucks air in and out. 'One last push when I tell you. Ready?'

Dressed in white, a tall figure turns towards me. 'What the hell are you doing here?' Eyes stare above the surgical mask. 'Get out!' And a brown hand waves me away, shuts me out.

'Now...!' And a faceless woman yells a child into the world.

The silence that follows drops me into a different time frame, when summer darkness had not been deep enough to cancel the view from the side ward where I waited for morning – waited for the surgeon to put an end to the life of the child nestling in my womb.

'I'll come for you when it's over,' said my lover. He bent over me, kissed my forehead. Nothing to do with desire, with his body joined to mine, with pleasure, with my head resting on his shoulder or my hand searching for his in sleep.

Robert wouldn't allow the foetus to grow to a baby because he had done with kids, his daughter, my son, sleepless nights, school fees, ballet lessons, rugby practice...

'Enough' he said, 'enough.'

'Excuse me.' A nurse pushes an over-bellied woman in a wheel chair. The mother-to-be grips her husband's hand so tightly the bones of her fingers turn ivory under the skin. She lets out a moan, arches herself back. 'Don't leave me, I'm scared.'

'You'll be fine,' he strokes her forehead, 'take deep breaths. It won't be long now.' He rubs the stubble on his chin, runs his hand through his uncombed hair, 'I won't leave you, I promise.'

Robert had left. I heard the biting of his tyres, the gravel they spat along the driveway.

'But I wasn't chained, you know,' I told the psychiatrist, ten years later, when sleep no longer censored dreams, and my unborn child begged me for a name. 'I could have got out of bed, opened the wardrobe, put on my clothes and left.'

He scribbled a few words on the yellow pad opened on his lap.

'But I didn't. I put myself first.'

'Did you?'

I couldn't see his face. I nodded. 'I thought Robert for a husband would be enough, but...'

'Go on. But...?'

'I was wrong. I don't think he loved me.'

'He married you. Nobody forced him.'

'Guilt did it.'

'Does he know how you feel?'

'I've told him that I can't forget, that the baby lives on, that I see her sometimes, that I watch her play with a red ball in the park, that she looks at me.'

'How do you know it was a girl?' He always asks.

'I know,' I tell him. 'We never speak. The mother she's been given calls to her. "Come to Mummy," she says. "Play where I can see you," and the way she stares at me I know; I know she is afraid I might hurt her child, or take her away.'

'And would you?'

'Would I what?'

'Take someone else's child?'

'No. I am the one who should be punished.' When I looked in the mirror above the fireplace, I saw I was crying. I dab my cheeks with a crumpled tissue I drag out of my pocket.

My shoes squeak on the yellow tiles. Perspiration crawls on my skin under the silk blouse I changed into before I left the house. I'm worried I might be leaving a trail of sweat behind me, that others will smell my fear. A man bumps into me, and his elbow catches mine. 'Sorry,' he mumbles, 'sorry,' and I know he's not because of the untidy bunch of red roses he clutches to his chest. 'It's a boy!' he tells me, 'a boy!' Tears edge his smile. A flower falls to the ground, and I'm left picking up a rose. I lean against the wall and suck drops of blood from my finger.

'Are you all right?' A hand rests on my shoulder. I must have gone pale because the nurse asks what's wrong.

Everything. But I tell her it's only a thorn, and I'm tired, and I can't stand the sight of blood, and don't worry about me, I'll be fine. She pats my arm and walks away.

I shouldn't have come. I should not be here. It's not my place. Not even Robert had the impudence to ask me to come and face his first grandchild. I wish he had. I wish it was the resentment bruising my memories, not me.

'I'll be late,' he said this morning over the locks of his briefcase biting shut, 'a dinner I can't get out of. Give me a call if there's any news from Helen...'

'About the baby, you mean?'

'Yes, the baby.' His lips couldn't help smiling the soft syllables.

'Don't wait up for me,' and the front door clicked shut.

I did wait, but not for him. Rather than go to bed I chose to curl up on the settee and do battle with my thoughts while the wind tapped branches against the lounge windows.

When the phone rang I let the jingle ricochet from one dark curtained room to another. My recorded voice invited a message: 'Jeremy here. Helen and I have a daughter. Alicia is seven pounds and three ounces, and beautiful.' Taut as a violin string the voice of my son-in-law by marriage faltered. 'Mother and child are doing fine.' His joy hummed on the line. 'I'll call back later.' He fumbled with the handset, and cut off the connection.

A pain stretched from my abdomen to my throat. Then came the panic, the feeling that I had strayed too close to the edge. Despite the heat from the fire I was short on warmth as if my physical being needed to reflect my inner thoughts. I sank deep in the thick cushions.

Expecting the news had been nothing compared to the shock of hearing it. Now I had to move on and settle with the pain. My pain. I could have pretended the words had not been spoken, that the sound of the television had drowned the ringing, that the machine flickered its small red eye in undisturbed darkness. No, the message wouldn't let me. It hopped about in my head, and the words turned dancers, the choreography simple at first until the syllables separated, jumped about, reassembled, threatened. Then Alicia grew features I recognised; she took on her mother's high cheek bones, a straight nose like her father's, Robert's determined chin, and from Helen's mother the deepest of blue eyes.

I fast-forwarded to the christening, to Robert standing by his ex-wife, so close their lips were almost touching, to the grandparents in a huddle around the baptismal font, heard their words giving thanks to the Lord for granting them a kind of eternity.

Then we would adjourn for lunch in a country hotel; there would be food and wine and coffee and liqueurs, after dinner mints, and speeches and the resemblance competition, where only the genetically linked can play, followed by the "do you remember" game, and Robert, and Helen's mother sitting side by side in renewed friendship. Or more. I saw the way they hugged the other night when she called to collect the pram I'd bought for their unborn grandchild. I saw him caress her cheek, squeeze her hand, smile; like they belonged with each other in a way Robert and I never will.

So what am I doing outside delivery room six? On the door a pink-stencilled rabbit bares his teeth at me. The real threat sleeps inside, a child not yet three hours old. I press my emotional finger on the wound, the way my tongue can worry an abscess on a diseased gum. It's bearable. Just. I push the door open. The moment takes on a depth. I plunge in, my breath snags. I won't stay long. I just want to take a look at the enemy before I leave, then I'll go home, pack a small case, drive to the motel on the outskirts of town, and decide whether to stay or leave Robert to his family.

A whimper disturbs the overheated air. There is the click of a pen. A young woman smiles in my direction. 'Congratulations,' she says.

I turn around. She can't be speaking to me.

She bends over a plastic cot, 'Alicia, look who's come to see you,' straightens up, invites me to get closer. 'She's fast asleep. It's hard work coming into this strange world.' Her hand rests on the child's head. 'Is this your first?'

'Pardon?'

'Your first grandchild?'

'Grandchild?' The word takes me by surprise. 'No, she's not...' And because Dr Jennings – her name hangs loosely from the lapel of her white coat – looks worried, I lie. 'No, I suppose...I mean...yes.'

This time she laughs out loud. 'Don't worry, I've known grandparents pass out with shock or dance around with excitement. One even smuggled in a bottle of champagne!'

She turns back to Alicia. 'Now young lady I need to have a good look at you.'

'Is anything wrong?' My voice doesn't sound my own.

'No, just routine.' She picks up a pink folder from the table against the wall.

'We'll ask Grandma to do the honours, shall we?'

'I can't...' meaning the baby isn't mine to hold.

'Don't worry, she won't break.' She pulls away the pale lemon cellular blanket, and reveals Alicia lying on the white sheet, arms stretched back on either side of her head. She wears nothing but a disposable nappy taped round her waist, and loose on her tiny wrist a pink plastic bracelet, the jewellery of the newborn. Her chest barely registers her breathing, and I guess at the silent puffs through the petal thin lips. She frowns, chases a dream – if newborns have a world to dream about – kicks a foot in the air then the other. Her hands fist and let go. I study the pale blue lines that web her closed lids, watch her mouth pucker, suck, turn serious and all-knowing.

I rest my handbag on the floor, take off my coat, fold it over on the back of a chair, turn to the sink in the corner of the room, and grab a paper towel to wipe the sweat off my hands.

Images jostle with each other. In another time frame Alicia could have been mine. I pray my unborn daughter can forgive me and that she slept so soundly she knew nothing of the masked man who came at her with a scalpel. A blade slices the air in front of my eyes. Even closed they register the pain, and the throbbing spreads to the rest of my body, and it is as if the trembling calls on the tears of a dispersed sea that swallows my breath. I choke.

'Are you all right?' the paediatrician lays a hand on my shoulder. I breathe in the smell of antiseptic and baby powder, find it easier to say 'Yes' than explain how far I have travelled to stand by a plastic cot. 'It must be the heat.'

She walks to the window, releases the metal catch, pushes the pane towards the night, and a ribbon of cold air curls round my head. On her way back she picks up a plastic jug sitting on a side table, pours water into a glass tumbler she hands over to me. 'Drink slowly. Would you like to sit down for a while?'

'No, please, I'll be fine.' Which I'm not sure is true, but I have to say something, just as I have to persuade my feet to carry me forward, towards the whimpering child, one step at a time. My thigh presses against the cot, my hands grasp the rounded edge, my stomach contracts. There is nothing graceful in the way I bend forward towards Alicia, neither in my body or mind.

I question what I want for this child, if I want anything that is, apart from preserving a safe distance between us. But now I watch myself slide my right palm under Alicia's head, and her pulse scuttles along my arm. Fingers spread open, my left hand slips under the infant's body, I lift her out, and hold her level with my face. I marvel that she can be both so light and so heavy. I am about to entrust her to the paediatrician when her pager bleeps.

'I've got to go. Shouldn't be long.' The young woman rakes her hair back in place with her hand, adjusts her glasses, hooks her pen in her top pocket, and just as the door is about to close behind her, suggests that Alicia and I should get to know each other.

'Is that wise?' I ask the infant, who whimpers. But I don't want her to wake up. Not yet. My arms draw her closer to my body, I press the small burden against my chest, accompany the lolling head to rest on my shoulder. Because Alicia fills the hollow place in me that has so longed to embrace a baby I forget to breathe. Confronted with her vulnerability mine bursts like a soap bubble filled with tiny rainbows, and I am surprised there is no crimson hate.

Alicia's heart flutters above mine. 'There, there, little one, all's well.' I pat her on the back. I coo, I speak words of unconditional love I thought forgotten.

I stroke Alicia's downy head, pat the little roll of flesh that pads the neck of the newborn, inhale her newness. And now comes the nuzzling, the budding caress of diminutive fingers against my skin, a wisp of breath, the hovering of butterfly lips. I close my eyes so that the birthing bed, the white sink, the regulation hospital chair, the room no longer exist. I shut out the whining of an ambulance, feet running down the corridor, a voice calling, a scream, and the world is just us, my granddaughter and me.

A Withered Rose

Hannah Knowles

To me cemeteries have always been cold, wet and bleak. My
first funeral was my grandfather's. January, 1947. The Saturday
before the snow came, and the sky that day was low, pregnant
with the snows that were to paralyse the area for many weeks. I
was ten years old. Old enough, so the family thought, to be one
of the black-clad mourners. I felt very important as I rode in the
first car after the sombre group of slow walking men behind the
hearse. I hoped that the on-lookers that lined the pavements,
as was usual in those days, recognised me, and realised how
privileged I was to be in the big Humber Hawk taxi.

When the time came for my grandmother's funeral I was much
older, and had by then attended many funerals and seen the neat
lines of gravestones creep further down the slope, making the
cemetery an even sadder place.

But on my last visit in June it was completely different.

I went because I wanted to. There was a compulsion that I had
never experienced before. Oddly, I wanted to visit my parents'
grave. For the first time since they were buried over twenty five
years ago I wanted to visit them and...I don't know...beg their
forgiveness, I suppose. Especially my mother's forgiveness.

I had hated her. She had ruined my life. Because of her, I had
to have an abortion. No, she did not make me do it. She did not
even know that I was pregnant. But what else could I do? I had
the choice of either putting her in a nursing home, and keeping
the baby which I was convinced was going to be the girl I so
desperately wanted, or I could terminate the pregnancy and keep
on caring for my crippled, bed-bound mother.

I was at the end of my tether. I could hardly think straight because of the disturbed nights. Goodness knows the district nurse had tried.

'Nurse Davies has left special pants for you Mum.'

'I don't need those.'

'They might help at night.'

'But we have the bell, you hear that don't you?'

Yes I heard it all right! Two or three times every night. Sleep was difficult to recapture after tending to her toilet needs, and the strident sound would shock me into wakefulness again.

'Are you going to try your new clothes tonight, Mum?'

'Clothes? You mean those pants? Of course not! I am not incontinent.'

'No, but the nurse thought if you...'

No amount of appeal could make her see that I needed a good night's sleep. Other ploys had the same result.

'But you know how painful it is for you to be moved. And you bruise so easily.'

'The bruises don't hurt. It is just that my skin is thin.'

Doctor Wise knew what I had to endure. He fully realised the implications when he rang me with the positive results of the pregnancy test.

'Discuss it with your husband. We can find a place in a nursing home...'

But Mum would not survive in a nursing home. She had had to be admitted for a couple of weeks when Dad fell ill. He had been nursing Mother himself, refusing all help. Then, it got too much and he had a heart attack. I had to drop everything at home and leave my husband to hold the fort, caring for our ten-year-old son as well as doing all the work on the farm single-handed. I looked after her while Dad was in intensive care, and for a couple of weeks until he was well enough to be discharged from the hospital. Mum had to put up with two weeks in a nursing home while we got the end room converted into a bed-sit for them. The idea was that I would be able to look after them and do some of my usual chores on the farm as well.

Or so I had thought. Mother's demands were taking their toll on me. Then, unexpectedly, I became pregnant.

The decision to have an abortion was the most agonising decision of my life; to terminate a life, not for my convenience, but because my mother's selfishness had made my life hell. And I use that word advisedly. Then of course there was the guilt. That was soul-destroying. I was guilty because of the termination. Guilty because I could not manage to do everything. Guilty because I resented my parents' disrupting my busy and contented life. Guilty because I was not as patient as I should have been. Guilty because I could not help my husband on the farm when he needed me. Guilty because my son had to take second place after my parents.

The guilt gnawed at my conscience, gnawed relentlessly, always there; a cloud obscuring any serenity that I should have felt. Even twenty years and more after they had been buried at the cemetery where I had attended so many funerals, the guilt was there.

I had not told anyone, but my husband of course, about the pregnancy. I had to make the decision on my own. I could not let anyone take the responsibility to make such a momentous decision for me. Whether or not I did the right thing, God only knows. He knows the agony I went through.

I had to tell Mother that there was 'a bit of woman trouble' and that I needed some slight treatment which would involve my being a couple of days in hospital.

'The doctor will send you straight home, and tell you off for wasting his time,' she said. 'There will be no need for me to go anywhere. We'll manage for the morning you'll be away.'

'Doctor Wise thinks that the hospital can give you some treatment, some physiotherapy or something...'

'They only want to experiment on me. They want me as a guinea-pig.'

She did consent eventually to spend a few days in the local hospital. But she insisted on coming home the same day as I did.

'I can't take up a bed here, they might need it for someone else.'

'Like me,' I thought selfishly.

I had nursed the grievance for over a quarter of a century, and now, all of a sudden I wanted to visit the cemetery, even though I had seen the grave countless times. I had acknowledged it every time I had had to go there, but I had not wanted to be there, to really visit it and contemplate.

It was the Easter service that did it. We had a weekend in the Lake District and visited a small church for Easter Communion. The priest had probably preached his Easter Sermon many times and from his monotonous voice, I suspected that he might even be bored by it. To illustrate what the Good Friday Sacrifice really meant he recounted a story about a bridge keeper whose job was to open a swing bridge to allow boats up the river and to close it for the train to cross.

One day his toddler son was with him and he was playing in the control room. The bridge had to be opened for a tall yacht to go up-river. Just as the yacht passed, the bridge keeper heard the train's whistle. Hurrying to close the bridge, he realised that his little boy had crept into the bridge's workings. What was he to do? If he was to save his son, the train would plummet into the river with a colossal loss of life. There was no time, he had to crank his wheel to close the bridge, losing his son, but saving hundreds of lives. That old man, like God, sacrificed his son to save many lives out of love for mankind.

On the way home, that story haunted me. Little by little, I could relate to that old bridge keeper. Was that not what I had done? Was it because I loved my mother so much I did not want her to suffer the indignity of being put in a nursing home? Yes, I had sacrificed my daughter so that one old woman could finish her days in the midst of her family as she wished.

I just had to visit the grave. I mean really visit. To spend time contemplating, to make my peace, to apologise for being so impatient. I had never put flowers on the grave – my mother did not want any flowers. She did not agree with placing expensive wreaths or sprays on graves to wither and be forgotten. She much preferred to take flowers to the living. I had tried to keep fresh flowers always in her room. But now, I just had to take symbolic flowers to put on her grave.

It was an extremely hot week, and I had been able to have a day free to travel the hundred miles or so to the family cemetery. On the way, I stopped in a supermarket, and bought what seemed to me to be appropriate – a pot of growing white roses.

I spent a long time by the graveside. There was no one about, only me, and a "lark in the clear blue sky". I had never experienced such a hot day in the cemetery. The sun's heat shimmered over the gravestones. I knew that the roses would not last, but they were not meant to adorn the grave. They were symbols of my guilt. I had endowed all my guilty selfishness, my impatience and my resentments into those roses. They were beautiful flowers, so white, so pure, each perfectly formed, the leaves unsullied by any pest. I laid them on the grave, and after a long wordless prayer, I left.

A couple of weeks later, I went to fetch the flower pot from the grave. The roses had withered as I knew they would. They were a pitiful collection of brown stems, tinder-dry leaves that turned to dust as I touched them and what had been perfect white blooms were now papery grey tissues. In that useless powdery soil, I could see all my guilt evaporated into nothing.

I took the pot home, and disposed of the contents except for one withered rose. This I kept and now it is lying beside my parents' wedding photo to remind me that my guilt has been lifted and that yes, I had done the best I could for my ailing parents in the last years of their lives.

I Am Three Mothers

Ruth Bentley

I am three mothers.

In the past I would have said I was the mother of three but now my children are adults, and if this is to be an honest account, then that statement is true. I do not know when I stopped striving to be the same mother to each of them; over the years they grew into such different people that the rule of trying to treat them identically disappeared. I only know that, despite the love, I cannot be the same person to all of them.

'You're the only person who can make me feel bad about myself.' Louise slams the phone down, playing the game we've perfected over the last few years. It's the way we each win the argument. Whichever of us can make the last dismissive remark and disconnect, has won. Except it's not a game. It's a campaign, a hostile confrontation where every incident, every quarrel, linked together, reach down the years – reach forever. The static drones in my ear. The frustration gnaws at my stomach in the same way I chew the inside of my cheek.

This time she's won. But in truth there are no winners. We both lose. Her statement brings the guilt to the surface and makes me question whether I was ever a good mother to my eldest child, this thirty-year-old woman.

I can't remember when it started, the shouting down of the other's voice, a refusal to listen. I only know that it seems always to have been this way; every argument the same. And over the last few years, when she has needed me the most, the precursor to the quarrels is similar: 'I need your help,' she tells me. 'Not your advice.'

So I keep quiet.

'You're not interested in anything I do,' she says.

Or I speak, carefully choose each word, knowing that whatever is said will be wrong, because the moment is wrong, until, exasperated that I am still treating her as a recalcitrant teenager, I tell her what I think. Why? Why do I question her actions? What right do I have? Why with her and not my two other children? I don't know.

We are unable to talk. There is anger between us and it seems to have always been there. Maybe it's because I can't make her life better than it is, without letting go of more of my own freedom. It is impossible to give in to all her demands. She is not a child any more, but still I allow myself to feel culpable. She blames me for all the wrong things in her life. I resent her because she never acknowledges that, as a mother, I have done the best I could.

And in writing that, I have suddenly realised that it is that barrier, that inexplicably shared antipathy that also chains us together. For a long time, as people, we have needed to be free of each other, to have space to grow, away from one another but it has not been possible. She has needed my help.

She has her own child, our grandson Joshua, born a month after his father walked out on them. At the time she was distraught and asked to come home. She needed me and I had another chance to be the mother she wanted. I grabbed the opportunity.

When our grandson was born, I was ill with breast cancer. Helping Louise gave me a purpose to fight the illness and staved off my fears. I buried the secret guilt I felt, that her distress had given me hope, by trying to let her have the kind of life she wanted. My battle with the cancer was intertwined with looking after Joshua when she was too tired, wanted some time out, wanted to party. My daughter's emotional need gave me strength to support and encourage her to regain her confidence.

That first year was the most peaceful I have ever had with my eldest daughter. We had a common goal: to love the baby she had brought into the world. Throughout her labour, I was there. I was there when Joshua was born. I cut the cord between my child and hers; a moment that should have bonded us for life.

But it didn't.

When Louise was born I swore that she would not have the childhood I had. She wouldn't suffer the abuse, the neglect, that I later learned was not the norm. Without example, I loved and learned to mother in my own way and I would do it in the same way again. Or would I? Even now, I still doubt myself.

Only three when the twins arrived, Louise struggled to deal with the attention suddenly diverting from her. She and I had times on our own. I did everything the "experts" suggested, yet I know I failed to make her feel special. Over the years her refrain has been, 'You've got Dad, Marie and Paul have got one another. Who have I got?' No answer was good enough, so when our grandson was born, although she hadn't chosen to be a single mum, here was a person who she saw as "hers", who belonged just to her.

But even though she wanted to be his mother, she also told me that, at twenty, she needed a social life. As a result, for the first two years I was with him every day. Then she moved to a home of her own. But I was still needed and saw him constantly. I know I have become too involved, but looking back, and knowing myself, I realise it was inevitable. It has been a re-run of my own motherhood, like having a fourth child.

Was it that I enjoyed the influence that I had on Louise – seemingly for the first time? I don't know, but, thinking about that, I feel I am uncomfortably near the truth. Louise wanted help, but not interference, encouragement but not intrusion. I've trodden a fine line, often I've got it wrong and looking back to her earlier years, I can see the recurring pattern of misunderstandings and her cries for attention.

Because of her difficult behaviour we were asked to remove her from so many activities and places. Week after week she caused chaos in Sunday School until the teacher couldn't cope any more. In the Brownies she threw tantrums because she didn't like the group she had been put in. She fought in dancing classes and sat in sulky silence throughout three piano lessons before the tutor gave up. She told me she wanted to do these things, but they were never what she expected. We planned outings, just for the two of us – but with a husband, two other children and a part-time job, these occasions were limited. She knew and resented that.

I lost count of the number of times I was called into school to discuss her disruption to the classes. Faced with her defiance and sulking, I gave up trying to reach her, even though (or to be honest, *because*) I knew that, for her the attention, any attention, was better than being ignored. Our relationship deteriorated even more in her teen years. Truancy and rebellion turned our home into a battlefield. Each of us fought for the upper hand. She ran away, but made sure we knew where to find her. She was caught shoplifting, stayed out beyond her curfew until she eventually stayed out all night. To my shame, I slapped her. She hit me back.

Expelled from school, she tried various jobs over the next couple of years, but soon lost interest. Then she found work in a holiday camp. Accommodation came with the job and she left home at nineteen. It was there she met Joshua's father. Within two months she was pregnant. Eight months later, she came back home.

Today, we haven't spoken for a month and she has stopped a lot of my contact with Joshua. Over the last year, things have deteriorated. Louise separated from her partner of four years and bitterly refuses to let her son see him, even though the two of them were very close. Besides my husband and son, Steve was the only male constant in Joshua's life for all that time. The break-up seemed to be a joint decision, but she was hurt and within weeks met and became totally involved with someone else. Twelve months on, she is now engaged to yet a different man, someone who has little interest in her son. All her life she has developed relationships rapidly and this has always worried me. But now I am angry. I see Joshua's pain and bewilderment. He talks to me. I hear him hurting and I cannot stand by and say nothing.

So I said too much. We had another argument and now we have this silence and it breaks my heart. She is my daughter and I love her, so I will pick up the telephone and try again. Tomorrow.

The difficult relationship I have with our elder daughter is in complete contrast to the one with our son, Paul. Both as a child and as a man he has been easy. His sense of humour is infectious and he is good company. He makes me feel that whatever I do is all right with him.

But this love I have for him has been reinforced by confronting the possibility of losing him, the knowledge that he could have died before me.

It was the week before Christmas 2000, the 19th December, when he told me he had testicular cancer. Tall and bronzed from a year's backpacking in Australia, at twenty-three he looked the picture of health, but for once his face was serious. He had been to our local GP, taking with him the scans he had had taken when he was in Brisbane. Our doctor had said he would arrange for a hospital appointment.

I couldn't take it in. Apparently he'd known he had cancer for some months whilst in Australia, and kept it to himself.

'Why on earth didn't you tell us?' I asked him.

'You'd have made me come home and I still had a lot to see,' he answered simply. 'And you got over cancer. I'll get over this.'

All the time he was in Australia he kept in touch by letter and telephone. He sent photographs and details of where he was. Yet he kept that secret and even now, when I study the later photos, when he knew he was ill, I can't detect any change, any worry in his eyes. One, with Ayers Rock in the background, is a close-up of him sitting in the middle of a group of friends. Every one of them is laughing. Why didn't I know he was ill – shouldn't I have been able to tell?

Within two days we were given an appointment at the University Hospital, Cardiff, and although I was relieved that he would see the specialist so quickly, I also knew that our son had a fight on his hands.

Later, as my husband and I sat in the corridor, the registrar came to see us. His face was serious. I felt sick. Paul needed immediate surgery, the removal of the right testicle and then chemotherapy. He'd advised Paul to bank sperm in case the treatment made him infertile. He would have blood tests and chest x-rays to see how far the cancer had travelled. Walking down those long corridors everyone else seemed so casual. I remember thinking, couldn't they see our world had shuddered to a halt? The nurses were kind, but matter-of-fact – how could they be anything else? They told us we would be notified of the day of the operation. There was a possibility of delay because of the Christmas holidays.

I wanted to scream, 'Now! Do it now. Get this thing out of my son.'

Paul was admitted to hospital the day after Boxing Day. He was very calm, too calm really. Even when we were given the news that the cancer had spread to his kidneys, he was unruffled.

For the first time in his life I didn't know how to talk to my son. There were no words that were not trite. Late that night, as I walked from one pool of artificial light to another, across the deserted icy pathways of the hospital grounds, to the family room I had been allocated, I was conscious that I was walking that tightrope of caution once more. But this time it was for our son, and not Louise. And this time the explosion of angry words would be a relief to hear.

They never came.

After the operation, we were told that he would need extensive chemotherapy and within a fortnight he was fit enough for his first session at Velindre Hospital, just outside Cardiff. The first day was taken up with blood tests, meetings with doctors, x-rays, walking from one room to another. Eventually Paul was allocated a bed and the treatment began. The image of him hooked up to an intravenous drip will stay with me forever, but still we laughed and joked. Only on the way home did I give in to tears, the long journey giving me too much time to relive memories of his childhood.

The next four months were horrendous for him and silently I raged – against the gods, fate, whatever. Sessions of the chemotherapy produced nausea, fainting attacks, loss of his hair and a high temperature. Each time, his blood count plummeted and he had to be admitted to hospital as an emergency. Each time he had to be in isolation, in a side ward. The joking had long since stopped, but still there was no anger from Paul. Instead he was depressed. I was depressed. We sat in silence. I held his hand.

Eventually his natural optimism returned. Determined to carry on a normal life, he applied for a job at a local leisure park. But on the morning of the interview he woke up with a temperature again. He should have been admitted to hospital at once but insisted that he went to the interview first. I watched him stride into the building and waited. Half an hour later he came out. As he got into the car he said with a grin, 'Well, I got the job,' then visibly wilted. 'Let's get to the hospital.' Again they put him in isolation.

We almost lost him that time. That fear has never left me.

Four weeks later, before the last chemotherapy, he began work and met Rachel. As the months passed they became close friends. She was a great support to him and gave him hope for the future. I will always be in her debt for that and am very fond of her. She came to live with us and a year later they moved into a flat together. Early last year they married.

On the 10th December 2005, they had a baby boy, a cousin for Joshua.

I am also lucky with my relationship with Paul's twin sister, Marie. Although she left home ten years ago and now lives in Cardiff, she visits often. We talk almost every day and we share the same sense of black humour. She expects nothing more from me than empathy and a sympathetic ear when she needs one, and gives the same. It is a rapport that frees both of us from obligation, yet holds us together. We are honest with each other and I value that. Even on the rare occasions when we argue, things don't degenerate in the same way as they do with Louise. More often than not, we agree to disagree and change the subject and, if something rankles, it's discussed when we've had time to think.

Over the years our relationship has evolved into companionship. Yet there are clues that make me realise there have been times when I could have been more aware of her needs. A quiet child who worked and played with equal determination, I always assumed the role of easing the pressure that she generated for herself, to reassure her that winning, being first, was not always necessary. Though I watched her with a sense of pride and admiration as she worked through school and university, I was determined not to be a pushy mother. At the age of twenty-eight, she still has a strong competitive streak that drives her to success in her field of work, and I am still urging her to relax. But sometimes, when she is striving for perfection and is exhausted, there is a brittleness to her that I recognise as a trait from her childhood and occasionally I wonder what else I could have done to help her cope, what else I can do now.

And then I think the only answer can be to reflect her behaviour towards me, when I was ill; to love and support in my own way. And to realise that is all I can do.

I know that with both Paul and Marie, the accounts of how my life still intertwines with theirs is an examination that is neither as long nor as complex as the story of the one I share with Louise. However, I am aware that their growing into adults was set against the background of our turbulent relationship and there is always that guilt. But there is no going back, so I try to believe that I did my best for them when they were younger. They seem to have accepted that and moved on. And, when I am with them, I am content in a way I feel I never will be with Louise.

But is that what it is all about? Is my love for my children measured only by comparing the degree of trouble, the amount of heartache, they have given me? Shouldn't it go beyond that? Is that why I feel my role of a mother is still incomplete?

And why I am three mothers?

Confessions of a Pushy Parent

Mel Parks

I had one of those conversations today when the truth nearly came out. I was in the checkout queue at the supermarket, balancing a basket of recycled wet wipes, biodegradable nappy sacks and sugar-free biscuits on the hood of the pram, when Ioan started saying 'Cake, cake, cake.' I offered him a chunk of peeled apple from a Tupperware box in my bag. He waved his arms around frantically, sucked in his breath ready to let out a yell that would be heard at the bakery counter and creased up his eyes ready to squeeze out a tear. The woman in front of us turned round, gave him a big exaggerated smile and an equally big, exaggerated hello. And he smiled back, the white of his four new teeth gleaming.

'How old is he?'

'Just over a year.'

'What's his name?'

'Ioan.'

'That's a name you don't hear much.'

'It's Welsh.'

'Really? I've never been to Wales. Awful isn't it? Who's Welsh, then?'

'Me.'

'You don't have an accent.'

'No. I've lived in England for a long time. His dad's English.'

'Half-English, half-Welsh. Who's he going to support?'

'Wales, of course,' I say. Then, 'No, really. It's up to him who he supports.'

'Yes, of course.'

'But I'll be disappointed if it's England.'

The words 'Support? Don't you mean play for?' almost escaped from my lips as I laid each item in my basket neatly on the conveyor belt. The truth is that underneath my liberal, I'll-be-delighted-with-everything-my-child-chooses-to-do façade, I am a competitive, pushy parent. One of the worst. But worse than the worst pushy parents, I pretend I'm not. I use washable nappies because they help toddlers to potty train earlier. I was first in the queue for baby signing classes because American research has shown that signing improves IQ. I elbowed my way into music classes to help Ioan's concentration and rhythm.

When Ioan's hands were staring to uncurl, his eyes starting to open wide, and his skin starting to become milky white. I ventured out to the health centre for his weekly weigh-in. I unpopped his sleepsuit and vest, talking gently to him for the audience of health visitors and other parents. I laid him on the scales, adding four blue paper towels for an extra half ounce, and instead of waiting for the three beeps, I watched for the highest weight which flashed up as the numbers fluctuated.

As I filled in the chart and heard the health visitor ask me if everything was all right, I devised a new eating regime. I would stop off on the way home for a bag of pink-iced and chocolate-coated, doughy calories. Ioan would spend more time suckling, despite the Baby Whisperer's warnings about starting bad habits.

I sat with Ioan at my breast for more than an hour. Radio Three filled the room with classical music, and two pint glasses of water and a pile of doughnuts sat by my side. I tilted my head back, closed my eyes, lifted my feet off the floor and drew air circles with my toes. The biro dot that sat precisely two squares below the twenty-fifth centile, was becoming as indelible on my brain, as it was on the pages between the red, wipe-clean covers of the Child's Health Record. My baby was not born to be in the bottom twenty-five per cent of anything. Palm flat, I pushed down firmly on my breast to squeeze any last drops of milk into the eager throat of my featherweight son.

Weight targets were not only met, but surpassed by two mothers at our baby group. I call these mothers the Gina Ford girls. Gina Ford, the queen of routine and control was their mentor. Every minute which contradicted the charts stuck to their fridges, and the synchronised clocks in each room, was recorded in a dog-eared notebook. Every secretion, consumption and playful gurgle found its own tick box in the same notebook.

I could not own a similar notebook. It would have been evidence. I kept Ioan's routines in my head. That way, only I knew how Ioan had refused to sleep that morning before baby group, and how he screamed in his cot for twenty minutes before I resorted to rocking him to sleep in his car seat. Elbow on knee, head in hand, staring at a milk stain on the carpet, the muscle in my arm was just beginning to ache when his eyelids finally closed. Five minutes later, a car door slammed in the street and he woke up, crying. I strapped him in the car, hoping he'd sleep on the way to baby group. He didn't. I consoled myself with the well-known fact that the more time babies are awake, the more they learn.

That was the day when a GF girl's baby fell asleep right there, next to her, in the middle of the room. In the middle of the room where there were eight other mothers and their babies, talking, laughing, cooing and crying. GF girl gave her baby his comfort cloth, laid him down on his back on a blanket and stroked his head. He fell asleep. I have to say that again. He fell asleep.

'That's impressive,' I said. I stood up, swaying and patting a tired cranky Ioan. I couldn't help but talk a bit louder. 'How did you manage that?' I said. Irritation crept into my voice like a dribble of milk on a freshly ironed clean black T-shirt.

'It's because of his routine,' she said. 'I've put him down at one o'clock since day one. So he knows now when it's his sleep time.'

I put Ioan in his car seat and dragged him closer. GF girl asked me if I wouldn't mind keeping an eye on the sleeper while she nipped to the loo.

Ioan let out a cry and I rocked him harder. The baby didn't

move; he just went on breathing evenly, with the comfort cloth draped across his cheek and snuggled into his neck. As I rocked the car seat, it got closer and closer. And I got closer and closer, until I was within touching distance of the baby. I looked around. The other mothers were occupied with their babies, talking about feeding and sleeping. I reached out and, still rocking Ioan, I slid my hand under the cloth and pinched the baby's cheek. Not hard. Not viciously. Just enough to wake him up. He started to cry as GF girl came down the stairs. 'Oh, hi, you're back. He woke up. What a shame. He was doing so well,' I said.

'Don't worry,' she said, picking him up and shushing into his ear. She looked at me as I had looked at the midwife who told me to relax, and offered me an exercise ball when I was in the middle of labour. At that moment Ioan's eyelids began to droop and finally closed. I slowed my rocking to a stop. 'Shall I put the kettle on?' I smiled.

The GF girls were the only two mothers who came to the group at my house after Ioan first started crawling properly. That's crawling on all fours, rather than dragging himself across the floor with his elbow as if he was slithering through the undergrowth. Ordinarily two mothers would not be enough of an audience, but these mothers are different. They know, to the letter, the developmental milestones their babies should be reaching. And so do I. They express their disappointment at each failed target. I don't need to.

The GF girls drank tea and sat their babies on the floor, where they remained. I handed round warm Welsh cakes, cooked on a cast iron griddle handed down to me by my grandmother, whose kitchen was always full of steam and fresh baking smells.

'No trouble. They're really easy to cook. I'll give you the recipe,' I said. The memory of Ioan crying while I jiggled him on my hip, and turned the soft, breaking cakes over with one hand was only just starting to fade.

I placed Ioan's favourite toy where he could see it, but out of his reach. I mentioned the sun starting to filter through the clouds outside, sipped my tea, and crossed my legs. Ioan pushed himself up on to all fours. My stomach tightened. I knew, and they knew, that crawling is vital preparation for future excellence in trigonometry and quadratic equations. He lifted his head and looked at me. I smiled encouragingly. He looked at the red turtle with coloured hexagons. I pressed the button to make it light up and play a tune. He wobbled a little, then crawled across the carpet as if he had no idea he was the only competitor in the race. I waited.

'Oh wow! Look at him! How long has he been crawling?'

'Oh, I don't know, a little while.' Since 4.20pm last Thursday.

'Right, baby, it's time for crawling practice. I'm not having her being one of those bum-shufflers.' The GF girl picked her baby up, and laid her on her tummy. As Ioan crawled around her, her legs and arms flailed. She may have been okay in water, but on my carpet she was going nowhere.

'She'll get there in her own time,' I said.

A GF girl said, 'At the eighteen month check...'

Another voice rose over the plastic tunes and American catchphrases. 'What, they have a check at eighteen months, I didn't know that. Did everyone else know that? Mel, did you know that?'

'Kind of,' I say, shrugging. 'I think my friend's baby's just had one.' I grilled my friend about what happens at the eighteen month check, but she was just sent a questionnaire. I asked her if I could have a copy, but she'd already sent it off. I asked her if she could remember what was on it. 'Oh the usual,' she said. 'Are you depressed? Does your child look at you when you call her name? That kind of thing.' I searched babycentre.co.uk, delved into my library of child development books, and interrogated my health visitor until the eighteen month checklist was built in to my developmental strategy and three-year plan.

'Well, at this check, the baby has to build a tower with blocks. So we're practising, aren't we darling? He's up to two blocks now.'

'Wow!' I said. 'Talk about hot-housing.'

Back at home, I got the box of blocks out that was meant for Christmas. Ioan was busy turning the television set on and off.

'Ioan, come and see what Mummy's got.' Ioan stood on a cushion and stretched as far as he could, balancing on his tiptoes like Beckham about to take a penalty, until he could turn the stereo on and off.

'Ioan, look at these blocks, aren't they fun?' Ioan didn't look. I held Ioan under the arms ready to pick him up, he straightened his arms and collapsed his legs like one of those wooden giraffes with a push button underneath, and slithered out of my grasp.

'What's in here, Ioan?' I opened and closed the box. Finally interested, he came closer. I gave him two red wood blocks. He dug his teeth into the top of one, leaving faint indentations and a bubble of dribble. He threw the other one behind him using both hands, and laughed. I built a tower using every single block, one-handed. I knelt up to reach the top, and as I gently placed the last block on the swaying summit, Ioan stuck his leg out, waved his toes and without kicking, just touched the tower with his foot, so it toppled timorously, block by block. He squealed, and clapped his hands. I lifted him up in to the air, and squeezed him in close to me. It marked the end of the tower game, but the continuation of my footballer fantasy. With leg control like that, my baby will be the next Michael Owen. Building towers is for squares, kicking them down is where it's at.

The Glimmer of Hope

Joyce Mollet

The plane came to rest and the seatbelt sign was switched off. I reached up for my case and felt the same as I had since leaving home, of being outside my body, an observer of these seemingly normal actions. In the last twenty-four hours, I had crossed from one side of the world to the other and not once had I ventured outside this tight little emotional cocoon that I had created for myself. I was in a place far away from any feelings, separated from myself, this person that I had, over the years, started to feel comfortable with.

The telephone call had come, as these calls always seem to, in the still of the night. The ringing pierced the stillness in its demanding, insolent way. Only unwanted, destructive news would force itself into a home in this way and at this time of the night.

'Come at once, son in intensive care.' There had been many more words, sentences, explanations, gentle phrases. But those stark few words, that conveyed all, were the only ones that remained, and they still played like a mantra through my brain as I walked out of the plane. Thankfully, all that I had brought was packed in the case that I now carried and I made my way through customs and out into the airport. Warm, welcoming arms embraced me and I thankfully wrapped my own arms around my friend of many years.

'I am so glad to see you Joyce, my dear, but I wish the circumstances could have been different,' Helen said, her voice thick with emotion.

I looked at my friend and with every part of myself tightly

under control I dragged out the words of the question I had to ask and have answered before I could move another step.

'Is he alive?'

'Yes, Joyce, he's alive.' And that was all I wanted of my friend at that moment, all else would come later. With this, I could move forward.

In that same condition of unreality I allowed myself to be ushered to the waiting car for the drive to the hospital and, not knowing how, found myself at the doors of the intensive care unit. I allowed Helen to wash and dry my hands, as she would a young child's and open the door for me to enter.

He lay perfectly still in the bed, the body of a strong and healthy young man. The only sign of injury was a wound on the side of his temple with evidence of three or four stitches. I realized immediately that the massive injuries that had brought him into the ICU were all within his head. Helen's words to me during the journey to the hospital now flooded my mind. 'Traumatic brain injury.' I saw the reality before me in the tubes, monitors, and machines managing all human functions and making my son's survival possible.

My child had entered an alien land and the way was barred so that I could not enter and join him there. He was lost to me, and suddenly, for no apparent reason, I remembered the greek mythology I had read as a child; of Demeter, who lost her daughter Persephone when, against her will, she had been taken into the underworld. I crumpled and wept bitterly.

In the days and weeks that followed I lived only in the moment, the life that I had been creating for my retirement put on hold and seeming a thousand miles away. And so, in reality, it was. A daily routine came into being where every waking moment involved my son in some way. I talked with Matthew about all sorts of things, news that he had missed out on, memories of earlier times, messages from his many friends now scattered all over the world and always with music in the background. Through it all Matthew lay still, locked away in some dark and hidden world.

'How about some relaxing classics this afternoon, Matthew?' I asked. 'The nurses would also enjoy that, don't you think? The girls will be in later and I know they will change the tempo for you.'

When visitors arrived, I would take the opportunity to leave the ward and return to my rooms to take a shower and change my clothes but I couldn't keep away for too long.

The nights were spent in the reclining chair, thoughtfully placed beside the bed by the kindly staff. These nights were always fitful and troubled. In different forms, the archetypal mother figure, Demeter, entered my dreams, and I followed this mother across the earth, while she searched for her lost daughter. In these dreams I saw the earth as a wasteland, neglected by Demeter who was devastated by the disappearance of her daughter.

One night I awoke suddenly from one of these dreams and the dreadfulness of my own horrific situation bore down on me like a rapidly descending avalanche. I picked up my coat and hurriedly left the ward seeking out the peace and privacy of the adjacent park. Standing alone under the trees in the soft light of dawn I heard the blood-curdling scream of an animal in pain and realized that the cry was my own, pouring forth from my upturned face. Turning my back on the hospital, I ran through the trees, on and on until my body would take me no further and I dropped to my knees shouting all manner of abuse to a god who could allow such pain.

Slowly, I returned to the hospital. Opening the door, my heart lurched and I had difficulty in breathing. The bed where I had left my son was empty. I grasped the end of the bed to steady myself. A passing nurse stopped and in a bright cheery voice said, 'Oh you'll be the mother of the brain injury. He's been moved. Come with me, I'll take you there.'

I followed, still feeling dazed, until we stopped at the entrance of a small ward and we both entered. The nurse turned to leave, but before she could, I blocked her way. I pointed to the boy in the bed. 'This is my son, Matthew,' I said. Then, with a sweeping gesture I indicated the machinery, the dials, the tubes and all that was keeping my son alive. 'That,' I said, 'is the brain injury.'

A new routine began to develop now that Matthew had left the ICU, but Matthew's condition remained unchanged. Nursing assistants were assigned to each small ward and I was glad when Jock, an elderly Scot with a mass of white hair, took over Matthew's daily needs. He chatted away continually in his bright cheerful way and Matthew's lack of response failed to curb him in any way.

'Now Matthew, my lad,' said Jock as he washed the boy's face and expertly shaved him, 'We're expecting big things from you today. Tomorrow is your birthday and your Mum expects some little sign of recognition. It needn't be a song and dance routine, we're quite prepared for you to make the running.'

I smiled and looked across at the two men, the younger one still and lifeless, the older one bobbing about and active in his tasks.

'This is all so incongruous,' I thought, but that is where my musing stopped abruptly for there was no mistaking it, Matthew's right hand had stirred. Jock and I stood perfectly still and watched as Matthew, eyes still closed, slowly raised his hand and with his middle finger raised gave that unequivocal and succinct comment on life. Jock and I looked at each other in stunned silence and then burst into uncontrollable laughter. Arms about each other we danced about the ward with Jock singing, 'Matthew gave us the finger, Matthew gave us the finger.'

Matthew has been in recovery for six years and is improving all the time. He has taught English in China and now lives in New Zealand.

Gloriously Grown Up

Christine Stovell

For years I just didn't seem to possess the necessary qualities to be a good mum. Good mums cooked nutritious meals of freshly prepared organic vegetables minced to just the right consistency. I lost my temper and actually tipped the cold lumpy mashed carrot rejected by my daughter *over her head*, leaving us both weeping with shock and frustration.

Good mums went to toddler groups, smiled at other women's children and uninhibitedly sang, 'Row, row, row the boat' with the actions. I hoped my daughters would sneeze, vomit or come out in spots. Any excuse so that I didn't have to sit in a draughty church hall making pointless small talk and trying not to grab by the throat any hapless child who snatched a toy off one of my offspring.

Good mums tiptoed into their slumbering children's rooms to surprise them with a gift from the tooth fairy. I said, 'There's no such thing. Here's fifty pence.'

'Stop expecting them to be grown-ups,' my mother constantly reproached. 'They're children. Let them behave like children.' But the problem was I didn't know how. I loved them desperately – and it was a kind of desperation rather than joy – but struggled to connect with them. Perhaps having my daughters one after the other simply overwhelmed me. Giving birth, I'd decided, was such a painful, frightening business that I would have to do it again quickly or not at all. Consequently, all I seemed to do was look at bottoms, change nappies and tell my disinterested husband, as he walked through the door, how many more mountains of poo I'd cleared up.

I had no experience of children, hadn't the slightest idea of what to expect and hoped that my maternal instinct would just come naturally. I longed for my first daughter to arrive, but when she did, I felt badly in need of an instruction manual. A degree was no preparation for her first bath. I was convinced that I would drown her or drop her and dash her brains out on the cold hospital floor. Every day raised new fears that I would damage the beautiful, perfect baby who was now my responsibility.

Looking back, my daughters' early years were a time of guilt that I wasn't doing the best I could for them and fear of what would happen to them if I didn't get it right. I coped with those feelings by relating to them in the only way I knew how – by treating them as miniature adults, to the frustration of both sides.

To add to my glowing maternal credentials, when the girls were barely nine and ten, I fell in love with another man. Not a toe-in-the-water kind of affair, but the full tsunami. It was during my divorce when I felt most guilty and afraid, that I got the best advice from my ballsy American female solicitor. Shutting me up mid-whinge about the effect it would have on my daughters, she said, 'The girls will be as good as you.' At that point I realised it was living with all my doubts and insecurities that would harm my children most of all. Instead of measuring myself against some totemic perfect mother I had to wake up to the fact I was all they'd got, and settle for being a good enough mother.

With every passing birthday I enjoyed the girls more. Okay, I hated all the parties and sleepovers that marked the occasion, though I discovered a hidden talent for knocking up creative cakes. But it just got easier as they got older. I'm sure my mother's observations about the way I tried to deal with them were true, but I only really relaxed as a mum when the girls were at an age where we could talk things through.

There's a line that goes, 'When they're little they have little problems and when they're big they have big problems.' But once you've opened good lines of communication you're halfway to resolving the big problems, even when you don't always want to hear what's wrong. Potty training nearly pushed me over the edge, but unsuitable boyfriends, nights on the tiles, university applications and driving tests have come and gone and my daughters are astonishing, capable and independent young women who have blossomed, despite my early botched attempts to raise them.

As a mother of adults, I delight in my daughters in a way I couldn't when they were small. Perhaps it is to do with not having sole responsibility for them, although there are a few roles I still retain such as "Health Guru", answering the phone one day to hear, 'Mum, something's wrong. I keep needing to wee, but when I try I can't go, or if I do it burns like hell.'

This from my daughter two hundred miles away.

'Stayed over at your boyfriend's?'

'Ye-e-e-s. So?'

'Men's halls?'

'Yeah. Had to sneak to the loo.'

'Okay. It's probably cystitis. See a chemist and if it doesn't get better, go to the doctor. Oh, and – '

'What?'

'Wee before and after you make love. It'll help stop it happening again.'

There is nowhere so quiet as an open plan office after a conversation like this, but who cares when your teenager confides in you?

I'm also privileged to be "Wart Hog" to them. Years ago, watching some footage of a mother wart hog defending her young from all comers, my younger daughter commented, 'Mummy, that's just like you!' These days I try to curb my instinct to dig in metaphorical tusks and not too subtly but effectively despatch anyone who hurts my daughters. But they know I'll always step in to protect them if I can.

I was hopeless when they were tiny children, but I adore my daughters now and revel in their company. Now that they are young women living away from home, I see less of them, but fall in love with them again every time I do. Walking through Cardiff with them recently I took great pride in the glances they drew from passing strangers and had to curb an instinct to remonstrate with those who'd been remiss enough not to notice their beauty, all that long gleaming hair and skin in its fresh bloom.

My daughters are courageous, happy to make their own way by themselves both here and abroad. They share the same traits of being self-sufficient, loyal and kind and yet my two peas from the same pod are completely different individuals. They are not yet so knocked about by life or worn down or disappointed that they've lost their sense of adventure. The world is waiting for them and that's what makes this age of being a mother so rewarding. They're setting off, gloriously grown up and it's a wonderful feeling.

Author Biographies

Ruth Bentley is a pseudonym. The author grew up in a small village in the Pennines and moved to Pembrokeshire in 1978. A founder member of the Tenby Writers' Circle, her work has appeared in previous Honno anthologies. She has had short stories, poems, plays, reviews and articles published throughout the British Isles. She has won poetry competitions, including the 2004 Roundyhouse Annual Competition and the Lansker prize for humorous poetry. She has just completed an MA in Creative Writing at Trinity College, Carmarthen and had a play performed in the 'Play Off' competition at the Dylan Thomas Centre, Swansea. She has completed two books for children and is currently working on her second adult novel: a saga set during the Second World War.

Paula Brackston's first book was an account of her horseback trek around Wales – *The Dragon's Trail*. She grew up in Wales, spent some years away and now lives in the Brecon Beacons with her partner and two children. She has an MA in Creative writing from Lancaster University and works part-time as a script reader. Paula produces short stories for magazines and has just completed her first novel. She also teaches creative writing.

Maggie Brice is a pseudonym. The author has lived with her husband and two children near the Gower Peninsula for the past twenty years. She works part-time as a library assistant where (when she's not scouring the shelves for her own reading matter) she loves talking to customers about their favourite books. The rest of her time is spent writing. She has had four books published but this is her first appearance in a Honno collection.

Jane Burnham has been living with her three children near Aberystwyth for over twenty years. She has spent most of this time campaigning for organic farming. With her partner she set up a 6 acre market garden growing a wide range of organic vegetables. A few years later she started The Treehouse, a thriving organic foodshop and restaurant in the centre of Aberystwyth. She is now enjoying the first few months of retirement!

Brenda Curtis has lived in mid Wales since 1985. Originally trained as a nurse and midwife, she has since worked in a variety of jobs and in 1998 gained an Open University degree in Social Science. Her chosen fields of writing are poetry and short fiction. She also derives much satisfaction from writing fragments of autobiography and *Nurses Move Fast But Do Not Run* was her contribution to Honno's non-fiction collection about the 1950s and 1960s, *Changing Times*.

Kim Davies moved to Anglesey as a teenager and has lived there ever since. She left school and worked in sports and leisure prior to spending several years at home raising her family. After her younger son started school she returned to the world of education, gaining a degree in English and a PGCE. Having taught at the local FE college for several years, she now works as a project co-ordinator at Bangor University. Now she has more spare time she is pursuing her interest in writing whilst also studying for a Masters in Creative Writing. This is her first published piece.

Dorothy Gilroy sadly died shortly after submitting *Dancing On The Railway Line* to Honno. She wrote the piece while in hospital, where she had been diagnosed with cancer.

Amber Fleetwood is a pseudonym. The author is the mother of a 22-year-old son and a 17-year-old daughter. When her children were young she used to write stories for their amusement and has been writing on-and-off ever since. She has had several articles published in magazines and is currently working on two novels and a short story. In her spare time she enjoys growing vegetables in her garden, making wine and going for leisurely walks in the Carmarthenshire countryside near her home. She also sings in a folk club and is learning to play the guitar.

Irene Janes was born in Merthyr Tydfil – born, if her mother was right, with a book and pencil in her hand. In 1970, when she was twenty years old, married and pregnant, she wrote to Marjorie Proops for advice on becoming a writer. Determination and life experience was the reply. But mothering duties took over and Irene's ambitions were abandoned. Now, at an age when you can fade or bloom, she opted for the latter and joined a local creative writing group. She writes for a Swansea-based news magazine and recently won first prize in a story competition entitled 'The Good Citizen'. Irene is proud of her valley upbringing and is sure there is a book in there somewhere.

Marie France Jennings is a pseudonym. The author was born at the foot of the Pyrenees and brought up in Paris by adopted parents. She first saw writing in English – an acquired language – as a challenge. She soon found it granted her a freedom not found in her mother tongue, which reflected a restrictive upbringing. Since completing an MA in Creative Writing three years ago at University College Cardiff she has been running workshops for the Lifelong Learning Department. Her work has appeared in various magazines, including *Cambrensis* and the *New Welsh Review* and she hopes to complete a linked-stories novel this year.

Carol King lives on the coast of west Wales. She and her husband, Ted, divorced when their son was five years old. She went on to become a special needs teacher. Carol didn't have any more children, but is now grandmother to Robin's two daughters. She is currently pursuing her interest in art.

Glenys Kinnock was born in 1944 and educated at Holyhead Comprehensive School and the University of Wales College Cardiff. She was elected to the European Parliament in 1994 and re-elected in 1999 and 2004. Prior to her election, she worked as a teacher in nursery, primary and secondary schools. She is married to former Labour Party leader Neil Kinnock, now Lord Kinnock of Bedwellty, and they have two children, Stephen and Rachel, and four grandchildren aged 10, 7, 3 and 18 months.

Hannah Knowles is a pseudonym. The author is very proud of her Welsh roots. She enjoys retirement and lives with her husband in an old stone cottage. Her garden, situated as it is between moorland and woodland, attracts all sorts of birds. Apart from gardening and bird-watching, she enjoys doing tapestry and listening to classical music. She has won numerous prizes for essays, for which she draws from her childhood experiences in the post-war years. Her ideal treat is dining out with friends and especially with her son and his partner.

Carolyn Lewis was born in Cardiff in 1947. Married twice with three daughters and five grandchildren, she now lives in Bristol. Writing since she was eight years old, her work has been published by *Mslexia*, Accent Press, the *New Welsh Review*, *Route*, *Libbon* and *QWF* as well as being included in two previous Honno anthologies: *My Cheating Heart* and *Changing Times*. Her stories have won a number of competitions including the Lichfield and the Phillip Good Memorial Prize and she has been shortlisted for the Asham Award and the Fish. In 2003 she graduated from the University of Glamorgan with an M.Phil. in Writing. She is currently working on a novel and a collection of stories.

Hilary Lloyd lived for fourteen years on a smallholding in the

Welsh Marches where she reared sheep, hens and geese. She retired to Devon in the summer of 2006. She has been writing seriously for ten years, has had short stories published in women's magazines and has won or been placed in several writing competitions. Her first novel, *A Necessary Killing*, was published in 2006 by UKS Press. She is currently promoting the book and working on her favourite medium - short stories. Her dream is to have a collection of short stories published.

Daisy May is a pseudonym.

Joyce Mollet was born and raised in the South Wales town of Llanelli. After forty years living and working in England, New Zealand and America, she returned to retire in her hometown where she has immersed herself in a wide range of interests including her two passions, local history and photography. She has two children, one living in California and the other in New Zealand, both adopted as babies from Bangladesh. In December 2006, the three made a return visit to Bangladesh, the first since the children left as infants in the late 1970s.

Eve Morgan is a pseudonym.

Mel Parks is a freelance writer and editor, specialising in children and families, after spending the past ten years producing magazines, leaflets, and brochures for childcare charities. This is her first piece to be published in a proper book. Having grown up in Wales, she now lives in Sussex with her English husband and two-year-old son who loves his Llyfr Geiriau. When not writing, and thinking up new plot lines using plastic pigs, sheep, and fire engines, she can be found baking with her baby group survival manual – Nigella Lawson's *The Art of Being a Domestic Goddess*.

Rosie Pearce was born on Dartmoor during the war and brought up in Sussex. She moved to Pentrecwrt, Carmarthenshire, twenty years ago. With five children and stepchildren plus six grandchildren, she worked as a laboratory technician, journalist and editor. Now a pensioner, she has recently started a part-time degree course in Welsh Language at Lampeter Univesity. Her interests include Greyhound Rescue, Merched y Wawr, cooking and foreign holidays. She is also, with her husband, a member of the Campaign for Real Ale. Spare time finds the couple growing all their own fruit and vegetables as well as tending other people's gardens.

Dee Silman was born in Hertfordshire in 1969 but currently lives in North Wales with her husband and two young daughters. Her short stories have been published in literary magazines and anthologies – most recently by Mslexia and Honno. She has also had some erotic fiction published by Cleis Press and Black Lace. In 2002 she completed an MA in novel writing at Manchester University. Four years later, she is near to the final edit of her book.

Christine Stovell lives and writes at Ferwig on the west Wales coast. Winning a tin of chocolate in a writing competition sponsored by Cadbury's at primary school inspired her to become a writer, an ambition she neglected for too long by going into local government and pretending to have a proper job. A member of the Romantic Novelists' Association, she is currently completing her first novel, *Fighting The Tide*.

Ally Thomas was born in Skewen. Married to Ken, she has two sons and a granddaughter. Graduating as a mature student from Swansea University's DACE in 2005, she won the Anna Marie Taylor Prize for outstanding contribution to the arts. She is a 'Martini' writer – writing anytime, anyplace and about anything. Keenly interested in politics, she is currently a local councillor. She co-wrote and sung lead as a mermaid in a musical performed in Taliesen, Swansea about a Wales Tourist Board scam. She is

Chair of Peacock Vein Script Shop and regularly contributes to 'Seventh Quarry' Poetry magazine.

Edith Thomas was born in Liverpool sixty-nine years ago. When she was nine years old she found she could read and began devouring books and is still doing so today. She married a Welshman and, with their five children, came to live in Wales in 1979. Their "surprise" sixth child was born in Carmarthen Hospital. Edith failed her O-level English Literature exam, much to her annoyance, but it didn't stop her from writing. She became interested in capturing her memories and writing down the bedtime stories she told her children. So she has attended, with great enjoyment, a number of creative writing and autobiographical courses since retiring.

Joy Tucker is a Scottish writer who has lived in Wales for many years. A former columnist and feature writer with the Glasgow Herald, she has had several short stories published in anthologies, newspapers and magazines throughout Britain, as well as having her work broadcast on BBC Radio 4. Her radio credits include children's stories and poems, some of which she wrote for her own son and daughter. Now she writes them for her grandchildren. She has recently turned to play-writing, with two one-act dramas produced at the Landmark Theatre, Ilfracombe, and one awarded Best Play in the 2006 Swansea Bay Film Festival. Joy lives on the Gower Peninsula with her Welsh husband.

Gabriella Walsh studied Biology at Oxford University, worked for the West Wales Trust for Nature Conservation, Ceredigion Heritage Coast and as a Countryside Management Lecturer at the Welsh Agricultural College and Aberystwyth University. She now practices what she learnt at the INPUT Pain Management course at Bronllys Hospital, seeking endorphins through having fun with family and friends, exercise and her role as an Independent

Living Advisor with the Rowan Organisation. She loves to spend time with her daughters, up to her eyeballs in glue and textiles and other motherly pursuits, hitting the trails orthopaedic style on her full suss mountain bike with her husband, quaffing coffee and roaming the hills with friends, seeking sanity through swimming, snorkelling and surfing and, last but not least, yoga. She occasionally makes time to write when the alpha waves are flowing.

Meg White is a pseudonym. The author is 44, has a doctorate in feminist theology and was one of the first women to be ordained in the Church of England. She has four children aged 11–19, who are home educated, and has written five books about home education and consent based parenting. She writes in her head all the time and at the computer whenever she can – articles, poetry and fiction. Her debut novel, *A Good Life*, and first poetry collection, *Particles of Life,* are both published by Bluechrome. She is currently seeking publishers for her second novel and first novel for teen readers and is working on a second poetry collection.

The Editors

Lindsay Ashford is the author of three crime novels, one of which, *Strange Blood*, was shortlisted for the Theakston's Old Peculier Crime Novel of the Year Award. A former BBC journalist, she was the first woman to graduate from Queens' College Cambridge, where she studied Criminology. Currently working on a fourth novel, she has also had short stories published in magazines and broadcast on BBC Radio 4. She lives on the Welsh coast near Aberystwyth and has four children aged eight, twelve, fifteen and seventeen.

Rebecca Tope is the author of twelve crime novels, including three based on ITV's 'Rosemary and Thyme' series. She has had a variety of interesting jobs, from ante-natal teacher to pig breeder. She has worked in every aspect of publishing and runs her own small press, Praxis Books. She is currently the membership secretary of the Crime Writers Association and lives on a smallholding near Abergavenny with her daughter and grandson. She has two sons and another daughter and two more grandchildren. She finds time for a lot of reading, travelling and gardening and is learning to play Bridge.

There was a huge response to the call for submissions, which meant that some tough decisions had to be made. The editors would like to thank everyone who submitted material for this collection and for sharing their stories.

Other autobiographical anthologies from Honno

Laughing, Not Laughing

Edited by Catherine Merriman

A unique collection of autobiographical writings from 26 authors writing about their sexual experiences – some blissful, some horrific, some farcical and all deeply personal. Compelling and deeply illuminating, Laughing not Laughing is essential reading for anyone interested in women's sexual lives.

> *'Illuminating, poignant, entertaining and "unputdownable", these accounts lift the lid on what Welsh women really think about sex.'*
> The Big Issue Cymru

ISBN 978-1-870206-62-4

Even the Rain is Different

Edited by Gwyneth Tyson Roberts

From sleeping in trees in Corsica to escaping Stalinist purges in Moscow. From Southern Europe to South America, Russia to Australia. Welsh Women write on the highs and lows of living abroad. These fascinating accounts of lives spent abroad in the past 150 years are a true celebration of the mix of cultural experience that makes the modern Welsh woman.

ISBN 978-1-870206-63-1

Short story anthologies from Honno

Mirror Mirror

Edited by Patricia Duncker and Janet Thomas

The wars between women – wife and mistress, first and second wife, mother and daughter, Welsh and English, the stay-at-home and the working mother – are fought out with fresh energy in this collection. Equally vivid is the longing – for lovers, fantasies, mothers, dreams, and for the other women we wish we were.

Includes stories from Patricia Duncker, Elin ap Hywel, Jo Mazelis, Ann Oosthuizen and Jenny Sullivan.

ISBN 978-1-870206-57-0

My Cheating Heart

Edited by Kitty Sewell

There's nothing foreign to the human heart, but there's lots that's forbidden and plenty that's hidden...

This anthology, collected on the theme of infidelity, includes work by Jo Verity, Jenny Sullivan, Ruth Joseph, and Melanie Mauthner, and each of the writers has fashioned a gem from the grit in the oyster of the human heart.

ISBN 978-1-879296-73-0

Available on-line now at www.honno.co.uk

ABOUT HONNO

Honno Welsh Women's Press was set up in 1986 by a group of women who felt strongly that women in Wales needed wider opportunities to see their writing in print and to become involved in the publishing process. Our aim is to develop the writing talents of women in Wales, give them new and exciting opportunities to see their work published and often to give them their first 'break' as a writer.

Honno is registered as a community co-operative. Any profit that Honno makes goes towards the cost of future publications. Since it was established over 450 women from Wales and around the world have expressed their support for its work by buying shares at £5 each in the co-operative. We hope that many more women will be able to help us in this way. Shareholders' liability is limited to the amount invested, and each shareholder, regardless of the number of shares held, can have her say in the company and a vote at the Annual General Meeting.

To buy shares or to receive further information about forthcoming publications, please write to Honno at the address below, or visit our website: **www.honno.co.uk**.

Honno
'Ailsa Craig'
Heol y Cawl
Dinas Powys
Bro Morgannwg
CF64 4AH